Sit Do... Guard!

*A memoir of growing up in a small Irish town
in the 1930s and progressing down a less
travelled road in the Garda Síochána*

Eamonn Gunn

First Published in Ireland, in 2013,
in co-operation with Choice Publishing,
Drogheda, County Louth, Republic of Ireland
www.choicepublishing.ie

ISBN: 978-1-909154-23-0 (Paperback)
ISBN: 978-1-909154-36-0 (Ebook)

Author Photograph: Courtesy Margaret Moore Photogenic

Printed in Ireland by SPRINT-print Ltd.

Acknowledgments

Thanks to my friend and neighbour Pat Byrne, a freelance writer, who first suggested that I should record some recollections of my experiences in the Garda Síochána and who edited my first drafts.

In particular I wish to thank Brendan Colvert for his perseverance in editing my manuscript and for his encouragement when my enthusiasm waned and my steps faltered.

I am grateful to Dominic Rooney who was a catalyst in my happy renewal of nostalgic connections with Manorhamilton and its friendly inhabitants.

I wish to thank Brian Smith of Dunlaoghaire for use of his material on Shanahan's Stamp Auction.

Finally, to my wife Rosemary for her support and patience as I struggled with this book and the computer.

Contents

Introduction

I was on vacation in Westport, Co Mayo in 1973 enjoying evening dinner with my wife after a tour of Scenic Achill Island. As coffee was served I casually exchanged words with a gentleman at an adjoining table, this led to a most enjoyable conversation while our spouses engaged, no doubt, in chatter about their wonderful men. We, as serving members of An Garda Síochána, had much in common, people we admired or scorned, current affairs, history and day to day experience, we were as described by Henry Wadsworth Longfellow 'Ships that pass in the night.' We did not meet again for many years until I became aware of Eamonn Gunn, the author of a fascinating story of anecdotal history a guide for posterity.

Frequently police meet people who are curious about what goes on behind the scenes, they are enthralled by stories of danger, investigations of serious crime, court room dramas and of course humorous incidents. This biography is not a Joseph Wambaugh's '*The Blue Knights*', or '*The New Centurions*', or '*The Choirboys*' but nevertheless when you start to read '*Sit Down, Guard!*' you will be reluctant to leave it down.

Eamonn Gunn was born in Pomeroy, Co Tyrone where two polarised communities kept an uneasy peace, Orange traditions and parades dominated society.

His childhood in a divided 'Border' Society was a curious mixture of acceptance and rejection. His father, who died at an early age, was in the Royal Irish Constabulary and later a founder-member of An Garda Síochána. His mother, a nurse, was unjustly deprived of her livelihood. As the story unfolds, we see the triumph of survival against all odds in times of poverty and alienation. Eventually, Eamonn joined An Garda Síochána. He gave a dedicated service to the State, which included diplomacy through the labyrinth of strained relations between poorly paid police as well as the intrigues of the Department of Justice and lordly Church dignitaries. He lifts the veil on aspects of Garda service and reveals the nature of police administration in its most vital role. His story outlines the difficulties experienced by the men on the beat to establish an independent organisation, with the help of Dr Garrett Fitzgerald, later Taoiseach and the Taoiseach in Office, Mr Sean Lemass TD.

The story is laced with humour, mystery, nostalgia and impossible characters that really existed. You travel to places rarely visited, and are introduced to the charms of location and the inhabitants. The humorous and sensitive recollection of 'life on the beat' in suburban Dublin in the 1940s–1950s encapsulate fading shadows of another time and place, as reflections on the changed scene brought about by passing years weave nostalgic patter of times past.

Let Eamonn guide you through an age that should not be forgotten. His orderly lifestyle is apparent in the manner in which he begins his memoirs by returning to the scenes of his childhood, this sentimental journey into quietude sets the scene for progress into an era that called for courage, resourcefulness and endurance. As Eamonn says, 'The past may be another country but for me it is also a precious place which I am happy to share.'

Brendon K Colvert

Chapter 1
Memoirs

Immersed in my retirement, I muse on memories from my life. Retirement is a turning point for everybody and at first it can be difficult to accept that a lifetime of commitment has come to an end. Fortunately, there are opportunities for the continuation of the camaraderie which has grown over the years, and I am grateful for the friendships which have withstood the test of time. There are, of course, regrets and sadness at the passing away of friends of my youth, but for now I am happy to occupy myself with these recollections.

I recall, from fading memories, times in the Garda Síochána, the long-vanished world of Sergeant Brady, and what passed for a police station in Ringsend. I remember the charm and beauty of Dalkey and its environs, the gallery of characters and the commonplace incidents from everyday life in very different times, 'Slippers' on his bicycle, Stephen and his petulant wife, Jessie, and Chauser who unpredictably crossed my nervous path, and my good friend John of DIY fame and his little work-shed that doubled as a shebeen.

My memoir begins with growing up in a small Irish town in the 1930s. There are memories of days spent fishing along the pleasant riverbanks and of a people who enjoyed the simple pleasures of that time. The consequences of the outbreak of the Second World War for a generation emerging from boyhood to adolescence will be touched upon, as well as recollections of the wartime scene in neutral Ireland.

It is, however, the recollections of service in the Garda Síochána that make up the major part of this memoir. At the present time the ethos and difficulties of the Garda Síochána are increasingly scrutinized, making the recounting here of the development of the role of industrial relations in the Force a timely contribution. In particular, the details of the state of industrial relations in the Force at a time of pivotal change in 1961, when men were dismissed for protesting the perceived injustices and poor working conditions, are important. The intervention in that dispute by the Archbishop of Dublin, Dr John Charles McQuaid, and the role of newly-appointed Justice Minister, Charles J. Haughey, lend historical importance to the narrative. Indeed the development of our fledgling Representative Association involved the participation of many persons who would prove to be pivotal in Irish affairs in later years. Our efforts to employ professional advisors brought us the help of Garrett Fitzgerald who later became Taoiseach. The then Taoiseach, Sean Lemass, who was also acting Minister for Justice, and the Minister for Transport and Power, Erskine Childers, also figure in the drama.

But I recount another, more vital, kind of drama – the humorous and sensitive recollections of life 'on the beat' in suburban Dublin in the 1940s and 1950s. These encapsulate the delightful, if fading, shadows of another time and place.

Chapter 2

A Boy from Pomeroy

My reminiscences of the Garda Síochána begin with a sentimental return to my native place – the little village of Pomeroy in County Tyrone. During the 1930s my mother returned from Manorhamilton to Pomeroy every summer. There she would stay with her sister Roseanna, whose husband had established a successful grocery and licensed business in the village. We usually visited during the month of July or August, depending on holiday arrangements for nursing staff at the County Home in Manorhamilton where she was matron. Throughout the years, we maintained a close family connection by these regular holidays during the summer, as well as by visits at Christmas and on other special occasions.

The ritual packing of suitcases preceded this annual visit. I became aware that the time for the family break was at hand when mother took down two large suitcases that were stacked on top of the wardrobe in her bedroom. I would not have seen these since the previous summer – and in those boyhood years that seemed a very long time indeed. With each passing day my excitement grew as I anticipated the coming weeks at my uncle's house in Pomeroy. It mattered little that he was not in fact my uncle, but my godfather. He was the man in my life, and I took great pride in referring to him as "my Uncle Paddy" whenever I got the opportunity.

The journey to Pomeroy usually took about four hours. We travelled from Manorhamilton to Enniskillen on the Sligo, Leitrim and Northern Counties Railway (SL&NCR); a small privately-owned narrow-gauge railway that connected Sligo to Enniskillen. At Enniskillen we changed to the larger Great Northern Railway (GNR). I was at first somewhat overawed by the impressive bulk of the GNR train. It had large gleaming carriages, with centre and side corridors that were not a feature of the SL&NCR, and it seemed as if the hissing and steaming engine was impatiently awaiting the arrival of a poor relative. Although making the transition to the Great Northern on the outward journey was always a matter of some excitement, it has to be said that the smaller little railway invariably had the reassurance of familiarity – like putting on a comfortable old jacket.

On our arrival at Pomeroy, there was always somebody from the family waiting to greet us – usually my young cousins. In those days, Jimmy Nugent was at hand to meet passengers coming off the trains with his horse and sidecar. Jimmy, small in stature but big in authority, took charge of all baggage and gave us firm orders on where to sit. With much delight we would scramble on to his high sidecar and sitting back-to-back eagerly await Jimmy's sharp command to his little horse.

A feature of most small towns and villages in that part of County Tyrone is the hilly nature of the terrain, and Pomeroy is no exception. That well-known ballad "The Mountains of Pomeroy" did not get its name without good reason. Up front, Jimmy perched on his driver's seat with his two Yorkshire terriers, one at either side, gently jogged his little horse up the hilly half-mile to the edge of the village. That stage of the journey, followed by the even steeper street to my uncle's shop, was the curtain-raiser to a happy and carefree month-long visit.

Uncle Paddy had started in business by opening a small grocery shop on the outskirts of the village. Being an enterprising sort of man, he was anxious to make progress, and when the opportunity arose he moved to larger premises on the Main Street. Here he built up his grocery business and branched out into the licensed trade.

My mother and I were always accommodated in the large front bedroom overlooking the street. The next morning, after our arrival, voices floating upwards from the street below were my waking call as the first stirrings of village life got underway. To my young ears the sound of those familiar accents breathed a sense of homecoming.

After breakfast in the large kitchen downstairs, a visit to the shop was my first priority. It was typical of village shops in those years, having two strong outer doors, which were closed and locked during non-business hours, and a glass panelled inner door with a quaint old wrought iron latch. The latch, when lifted, triggered a small bell within and gave notice of one's arrival. This device was not intended as some sort of burglar alarm, but rather as a means of ensuring prompt and immediate service for all. The shop contained almost everything from Kerry Cream Biscuits to sacks of flour and animal feed, boots, shoes, buckets and spades, as well as the usual range of groceries. Uncle Paddy's customers were mostly the neighbouring farming community, who expected and received substantial credit on their accounts, which were usually cleared after payment for the harvest had been received.

Those were the years of innocence. Only simple things seemed to matter – like rummaging, hopefully, in the top of the high kitchen press for whatever might be found. At first I needed a chair to stand on. As the years slipped quickly past, that familiar old press monitored my impatient rush into adolescence and, all too soon, almost before I knew it, there was no need of a chair.

Market and fair days were always occasions of greater activity for the household. Two large yards at the rear of the house became car parks for my uncle's customers. Here customers were free to leave their horses and carts under the supervision of Peter, who was employed by my uncle as yard-man for the day. Such days were important in the simple social life of those distant times. The little parlour adjoining the kitchen was seldom used, but it came into its own on these occasions. It was host to some of the older women who came shopping on those special days. Here they could chat and gossip with friends and neighbours, and renew old acquaintances – perhaps even over a glass of port wine. Those were not days of instant communication. There were no mobile phones, internet or television, and a market-day chat was an invaluable opportunity to catch up on all the latest news and family gossip. The sight of shawled women stealing quietly, almost furtively, into the parlour for a friendly chat is part of my childhood memories.

Sadly, there are less fond memories of Pomeroy. A ninety-per-cent nationalist village, it was in those days sometimes chosen by the Orange Order as the venue for their annual parade. It was customary for the parade to halt outside my uncle's shop and perform the drumming ritual. I still hear echoes of those drumbeats, as, surrounded by the silent apprehension of our elders, we peeped through the lace curtains at the sweating drummers.

My uncle's shop was, as I have said, situated on Main Street, which was the hub of whatever activity occurred in the village. For reasons that I cannot explain, there was a very large stone on the footpath outside the shop door. It must have been placed there at the time the shop was built. Its well-polished surface provided seating for half a dozen young boys, and was a regular meeting place during those happy summer holidays. Here I renewed my friendship with youthful companions from early school years, when I lived with my uncle's family prior to rejoining my mother at Manorhamilton. They said I was fortunate to live in the Free State, talked despondently about the injustices of partition, and fantasised about the future. Through the years that followed, our youthful perceptions may have dimmed, but thoughts of that big stone in Pomeroy recall words from the old Irish ballad "The Stone outside Dan Murphy's Door."

Chapter 3

Hands Across the Border

It seems that the hand of fate is destined to shape our lives. In my own case, events beyond the control of man set the course of life from the very beginning. Before I was born, a little house on The Diamond in Pomeroy, Co. Tyrone was the locus for those events. It was here that my maternal grandparents, Edward Kerr and Mary McCourt, set up house in 1880. My mother, one of their five children, would finally close the door on that happy little home in 1926.

Mother had married my father James Gunn from County Fermanagh in 1922. Their marriage was a happy one, but short – very short. He died two years later in 1924. With her ten-month-old son, mother returned to her old home, where her mother and unmarried sister still lived. Her father had died a year before, in 1923. Her two brothers, who had emigrated some years earlier and fought in the Great War with the US Army, were also dead. In the course of three years she had lost both her parents, her husband, two brothers and a sister – quite a challenge for a young woman still in her early thirties. Her one surviving relative, a married sister, Roseanna, living across the street, was her sole source of comfort in those difficult years.

My mother was a woman of great energy and determination. Just as well – otherwise she might have wilted under the stress of those successive family deaths. Educated at the local primary school, she later trained and qualified as a nurse in Belfast. It seems that nurses and policemen go together, and during those years she met her future husband – then a youthful constable in the Royal Irish Constabulary (RIC). Those were tension-filled years in Belfast, and the fiery young Alice Kerr from Pomeroy found a soul-mate in Constable James Gunn of the RIC.

Times were hard for most people in the 1920s. The Welfare State had not yet been established. Mother was fortunate in that she had qualified as a nurse before she married, but there were few opportunities in a small place like Pomeroy. Following the partition of Ireland in 1922, the new state of Northern Ireland was created. Politicians and officialdom were anxious to consolidate this new arrangement as firmly as possible and deeply entrenched attitudes abounded. Such opportunities as did arise were seized upon as a means of exercising power and political influence within the community.

My mother, a Catholic, had applied for a nursing vacancy with the Local Authority in Pomeroy. Though fully qualified, she was unsuccessful and a less qualified person secured the vacancy. Rightly or wrongly, it was perceived that mother's disadvantage was her religion. She was obliged to look elsewhere for employment, and fortunately succeeded in an application to the County Leitrim Board of Health at Manorhamilton in the Irish Free State.

During her first two years at the County Home in Manorhamilton she was obliged, due to lack of suitable accommodation, to leave me in the care of her married sister Roseanna in Pomeroy. My aunt had two children. My cousins were the same age as myself and were ideal little companions for this only child. Although sad at being parted from mother, I enjoyed the security and companionship of this happy home until the accommodation problem at Manorhamilton had been solved. Regular visits from my mother, when circumstances permitted, were the highlight of my days there. But, of course, the happiness then became part of the pain to come when it was time for her to return to Manorhamilton.

After two years, my enforced sojourn in Pomeroy came to an end and I went to live with my mother at Manorhamilton. She was, of course, delighted to be permanently reunited with her only child, and within the confines of that old place she found peace and happiness. I recall accompanying her sometimes during the course of her inspections throughout the building. In her freshly laundered, well starched uniform, she confidently strolled through the various wards and chatted with the inmates. I think that she was popular with most of them. Slight of stature, she was affectionately referred to as 'the wee nurse'.

During her years at Manorhamilton her thoughts were never far from Pomeroy, and she returned there whenever possible. Consequently, we never lost touch with our roots. I have abiding recollections of those long summer visits: the warm welcome, reviving friendships, the grandfather clock, the well-polished floors and the ever present whiff of camphor from the large oak wardrobe in our bedroom. Every time we visited I fantasised on its contents – the pale-blue uniform of an officer in the Garda Síochána. In boyish make-believe I tried to visualise the father I never knew. In the years that were to follow I would eventually discover something of the man who once wore that pale blue uniform.

The Wardrobe

Each year we came
One month to stay.
Old oak wardrobe in the room
Smelling sweet with camphor balls,

Life-like there each time I looked
A pale blue uniform on the hook,
With buttons gold and black Sam Browne,
Alone in sole command.

No mention of the owner then,
Dead at thirty-three
In nineteen twenty-four.

Born just one year before,
I did not understand.
They told me later who he was:
They told me he was Dad.

Chapter 4

A Letter from Michael Collins

My father, James Gunn of Oramore, Holy Well, Belcoo, Co. Fermanagh was an Intelligence Officer with the rank of O.C. of the 3rd Northern Division of the I.R.A.[*] As such, he was responsible for intelligence work on behalf of Michael Collins during the War of Independence. Father Caulfield, the local curate at Holy Well was a prominent and forthright supporter of Sinn Fein in South Fermanagh.[†] He was the recipient of instructions from Michael Collins to James Gunn, whose name could not be disclosed. Six months before his tragic death in 1922, Michael Collins sent the letter on page 11 to Father Caulfield at Holy Well.

In the aftermath of the 1916 Rising there developed an intensification of support for Irish independence, which culminated in the Treaty of 1921 and the disbandment of the RIC in 1922. Some members of that Force chose to join the newly-formed Garda Síochána – others chose to join the fledgling Royal Ulster Constabulary (RUC), but most took redundancy payment and settled into civilian life. My father, a friend and confidant of Michael Collins, chose to leave the RIC, which he had joined in 1912 and to cast his lot with the new Garda Síochána in October 1922.

The letter, along with a Christmas card from the year 1920 from Michael Collins, was given to me by my mother. The purport of the letter was that my father should continue his present secret work for Collins. In passing on this letter to me many years ago my mother

---

[*] The pre 1922 IRA

[†] See *The Fermanagh Story* by Peadar Livingstone

explained that my father had become increasingly apprehensive of his position and was considering resigning from the RIC. As can be seen from the letter, Collins was anxious that he should not then resign, and persuaded my father to remain in the RIC, which he did, until that Force was disbanded on 7th June 1922.

Michael Collins' Letter[*]

Various snippets of information percolated through family connections during my adolescent years, but my mother's recollections are the most reliable and most abiding. From her I gleaned that my father was chief clerk to the County Inspector at RIC Head Quarters in Lisburn, Co Antrim at the time of the shooting of Detective Inspector

---

[*]It was my pleasure to donate this Michael Collins' letter to the National Library of Ireland, Kildare Street, Dublin on 20th March 1997.

Swanzy at Lisburn on 22nd August 1920. Swanzy was the prime suspect for the killing of Lord Mayor Thomas McCurtain of Cork[*]. From my mother I learned that, as chief clerk, my father had access to the secret monthly code of the RIC and, consequently, to sensitive and confidential information invaluable to Michael Collins.

The final years of his life were crowded and hectic. He remained an IRA activist within the RIC until shortly before that Force was disbanded in August 1922. He married in September and joined the Garda Síochána in October of that year. He was appointed to the Garda Síochána on 30th October and promoted Inspector on the following day. He was initially involved in the administration of recruitment to the new Force and was later officer in charge of Westgate Station in Drogheda, Co Louth when opened by the Garda Síochána in 1923. He was subsequently discharged on medical grounds in 1924, and he died aged thirty-three years at the family home in Ora near Belcoo on 27th September 1924. He is buried in the family grave at Holy Well Church, Belcoo.

My mother received no financial support from the new Irish Free State during her long lifetime – and she never received a widow's RIC pension. She sometimes recalled that at the time of their honeymoon in Dublin in 1922, "he went off to meet some men one evening ... he never spoke too much on those things ... and returned with a gold watch they had presented to him." It was engraved as follows; *"To James Gunn, with the compliments of the 3rd Northern Division IRA"*

---

[*] See Tim Pat Coogan,. *Michael Collins* p. 124

Chapter 5

Tale of a Uniform

Sixteen years elapsed before the old wardrobe would surrender its nostalgic contents. As a teenager at that time living in Manorhamilton, I began to embrace the emotional desire of taking possession of my father's uniform.

It was 1940 and wartime restrictions were coming into full force. Since the first days of Partition there had developed an obsessive emphasis on cross-border traffic-control. Trains and buses were invariably stopped and searched at every border post, customs officials searched passengers and their baggage, and parcels sent by post were opened and sometimes confiscated or withheld until excise duties were paid.

All these years later, with the advent of open borders and free trade, it is amusing to reflect on the bureaucracy of it all. Perhaps it had as much to do with the political separateness of the two newly-created States as with anything else. In any event, the consequences were such that one invariably had second thoughts about bringing anything over the border.

In normal circumstances there should have been no problem with bringing home my father's uniform, as I could have declared it as a personal family possession. But such were the political circumstances of the times that, rightly or wrongly, it was decided to have the uniform clandestinely brought to Manorhamilton. As it transpired, this was silly and unnecessary.

The uniform was posted to an address in Belcoo, Co. Fermanagh, where an acquaintance had promised to secretly bring it over the border in his bonded lorry. Unfortunately my acquaintance not only got cold feet when the parcel arrived, but loud-mouthed the plan to such an extent that the local police were fed a story about a mysterious military uniform. The RUC, perhaps in the mistaken belief that they had uncovered a subversive plot, raided the address and seized the uniform.

I was devastated at his turn of events, but had little option but to call to the RUC station in Belcoo and explain my ownership of the uniform. Unfortunately, my visit was a humiliating experience. A not-very-friendly sergeant indulged in an inquisition about my father's background and his brief career in the Garda Síochána. Following serious questioning he left me alone with an abrasive young 'B' Special,* not much older than myself, who indulged in derisory remarks concerning the Irish Free State. About an hour later the sergeant entered the room and refused to return the uniform, saying that the matter was being further investigated, and I was obliged to leave empty-handed.

I later sought help from the Gardai in Manorhamilton, where the local Superintendent, the late Jim Bergin, was a man of courage and common sense. His sympathies, which had led him into the Garda Síochána in 1922, were similar to those of my father. A suitably worded letter questioning their authority and seeking the return of the uniform was sent to the RUC. Some weeks later, I was invited to the RUC station at Belcoo where a different sergeant politely handed me the uniform without comment or further questioning. And there the matter ended.

In fairness to the RUC, an unrelated event is worth recalling. It was over a decade later, in October 1951, when family ties drew me, once again, to a funeral at Belcoo. My mother and I set out on the journey at 6.00 pm. from Dún Laoghaire in a borrowed Ford Prefect. In those days it was necessary to have a car bonded for travel into Northern Ireland. My borrowed car was not bonded, but I had little option at that hour of the evening, as I was most anxious to arrive in time for the funeral. I put myself in the hands of fate and hoped for a satisfactory solution to whatever problems might arise when I reached the border at Blacklion/Belcoo.

---

* B Special were Protestant militia

Blacklion in County Cavan adjoins Belcoo in County Fermanagh, and the villages are connected by a river-bridge about four hundred yards long. The customs posts at either end were closed on my arrival at about 11.00 pm. Realising that I was prohibited from driving over the bridge with an unbonded car, I parked near the bridge and, as I was then a member of the Garda Síochána sought advice and assistance in the nearby Garda Station. As he stretched his recently-laundered shirt over two chairs before a blazing turf fire in the station day-room, the Garda on duty listened to my story: I had an unbonded car and an elderly mother, the family were well known in the area, and I had but two miles to travel to my aunt's home beyond Belcoo. Could he be of assistance with the local customs officers? Could he organise a local hackney car if necessary? No! There was nothing he could do.

I was very disappointed at his attitude, as I was quite sure that, had he chosen to bother, a little diplomacy on his part could have solved the problem. It was now past midnight, and feeling somewhat despondent, we decided that there was no alternative but 'shank's mare'. As we set out on foot, leaving the car at the bridge, we met a young Irish Customs Officer patrolling in uniform and a conversation ensued. He appreciated our predicament and personally would have no difficulty or concern should we decide to take the car into Northern Ireland. His concern was that the RUC, or Customs Officers in Belcoo, might prove a problem to us. The conversation concluded with, "Good night," and "Hope you manage somehow." And so he left us to continue our journey on foot over the bridge.

Having crossed the bridge, we were met by a young RUC constable and a senior man in plain clothes. On hearing our story, the senior man, who did all the talking, was most sympathetic. He had known my deceased relative quite well, knew where he had lived, and was quite sure that we should not be put to the unnecessary hardship of walking two miles uphill on a small country road at one o'clock in the morning. Certainly, he would rouse his local Sergeant and see if there were any objections to taking the car over the border. In the company of the two RUC men, we walked across the bridge into Belcoo, where the Sergeant was roused from his bed and, through an upstairs window, stated that he had no objections to our use of the car within his jurisdiction. Relieved and delighted, we thanked the officers for their understanding, returned to the car, and drove safely to my aunt's house, arriving there at about 2.00 am.

Now, if I thought that my problems were at an end, a rude shock awaited me. The following day in Belcoo, I learned that a hue and cry had gone forth concerning my illegal crossing of the border the previous night. The friendly young Irish customs officer, who had no responsibility for cars crossing into Northern Ireland, had noted the next morning that my car was missing from where he had last seen it the night before. He reported the circumstances of his meeting with me at the bridge to his senior supervising officer, as well as the local RUC station, pointing out that the car was now being illegally driven in Northern Ireland. This young officer had his lodgings, not in Blacklion but over the border in Belcoo, not far from where the local RUC sergeant also had lodgings. Belcoo is a very small village. Of course, the Sergeant, who had sanctioned my crossing the previous night, was now placed in a difficult position. He had been made officially aware that a car had been illegally taken over the border into his jurisdiction and he would be expected to act. For my part, I was totally embarrassed by this unexpected development. I was in a dilemma. The car could have been impounded in Northern Ireland, as an illegal import or, on re-entry to the Irish Free State, in the absence of a bonding document, have resulted in refused entry, or worse, it could have been confiscated. It was indeed a bizarre situation.

I contacted the RUC and expressed my regrets for any embarrassment that might have been caused. As far as I can recall, their attitude was that the matter was really of more concern to the Irish customs than it was to them. In other words, they were turning a blind eye to what was technically a breach of the law on my part. The matter was finally resolved by my attendance at the Irish customs post that night. Before the senior Irish customs official, accompanied by his junior officer and two RUC sergeants, in what amounted to a sort of court-martial, I was severely chastised for my alleged irresponsibility. My feelings were a mixture of embarrassment, humiliation and anger.

Embarrassed that a member of the Garda Síochána should find himself in such circumstances, humiliated that I should feel as if I were a criminal pleading for mercy, and angry at the young customs officer who had so broken his word.

In hindsight, I am satisfied that the senior customs officer, called so unnecessarily to pass judgment on a member of the Garda Síochána in the presence of the RUC, was saying no prayers for his youthful subordinate. As far as the RUC were concerned, I have nothing but praise for the manner of their involvement, both on the bridge when they encouraged me to take my car, and later in the customs post where they actually pleaded my case. Happily for me, there was an Irish solution to an Irish problem.

> *When all the world is young, lad,*
> *And all the trees are green;*
> *And every goose a swan, lad,*
> *And every lass a queen;*
> *Then hey for boot and horse, lad,*
> *And round the world away;*
> *Young blood must have its course, lad,*
> *And every dog his day.*

> *When all the world is old, lad,*
> *And all the trees are brown;*
> *And all the sport is stale, lad,*
> *And all the wheels run down,*
> *Creep home, and take your place there,*
> *The spent and maimed among;*
> *God grant you find one face there*
> *You loved when all was young*[*].

---

[*] "When all the World is Young, Lad," Charles Kingsley

Chapter 6

Back to My Roots

It was early August, and the weather was kind as the morning train sped towards the city through the suburban landscape. The Sealink ferry, escorted by screeching seagulls in search of breakfast, was gliding into Dún Laoghaire harbour. The smoking Electricity Supply Board (ESB) chimney stacks with their red and white collars surrendered their silent vigil to the approaching dawn. The three spires of Dún Laoghaire receded further into the glowing morning skyline; my thoughts were of the long journey ahead. I was taking my first steps in search of a vanished past – a nostalgic return to a small country town in the west of Ireland, the nursery of my youth and adolescence – not so much to a place as to a time of growing up. The hidden urge to return to my roots had finally triumphed.

As the wonderful panorama of Dublin Bay unfolded, thoughts of my ultimate destination contrasted sharply with my immediate surroundings. The tightly-packed commuters: the *Financial Times* man, the fashionably dressed young women sporting the latest in skirts and brief cases, clean-cut men, rolled-umbrella men, youths with shaven heads and silver earrings were crammed together in silent isolation. This contrast with my ultimate destination whetted my appetite for my mission – the distant west of Ireland seemed more inviting than ever. At Connolly Station I boarded the Sligo train and contemplated three hours of travel.

It seemed particularly apt that the western railway line should be served by ancient rolling stock, the grimy windows and the useless public address system belonged to another age. I resolved not to engage in conversation with fellow travellers but to observe the passing scene as we sped onwards through the quiet morning countryside. The lush seasonal growth and the occasional field of rushes evoked forgotten memories. The neglected old railway buildings were a stark reminder of the changed times, as was a countryside peppered with drum-like plastic silage bales – I yearned for the little golden haycocks, which I associated with the steam trains of my youth. The changing landscape was fascinating, and with the arrival of the tea trolley a sense of homecoming embraced me.

As we sped onwards I fell to musing on the purpose of my journey. Perhaps I was foolishly being swept off my feet on a tide of emotion? I could not explain this strange allure, which had directed my determination to revisit long neglected scenes. Three score years had elapsed since life began for me at what was the bedrock of my dreams. Undoubtedly, the winds of change would have dusted over much I had known, but memories had survived, and now sought empathy with thoughts of what lay ahead.

The earlier veils of misty rain had given way to a colourful skyline, as the sunshine glistened through the speeding hedgerows. I had belatedly awoken to the delights and benefits of public transport and could now take a leisurely laid-back view of the passing scene. A lone horse stood rigid, alerted to the passing train, a sculptured horseback rider commemorated times past, silent church spires looked down on a deserted village football field, and a white blossomed potato patch contrasted colourfully with ragwort gay in yellow head-dress.

At Ballymote some passengers boarded the train, while a few alighted to the welcoming attention of a black and white collie dog, whose presence I conjectured was part of the daily station routine. On arrival in Sligo I made my way to the bus station where I intended to board the bus for the small market town of Manorhamilton, nestling some sixteen miles away in the pleasant hill- country of North Leitrim.

It was a road I had first travelled on the old Appleby Bus Service of the 1930s. For young boys living in Manorhamilton in those days, a bus ride to Sligo was a rare outing indeed. A matinee visit to one of the local cinemas was usually the reason for such a journey. We would have considered the trip almost akin to travelling to Dublin or Belfast in later years. The Sligo terminus for Appleby's bus was at Gray's Inn, a small tea-room and newsagent's shop near the river bridge. From there we would sally forth to sample the wonders of Woolworths, before assembling at one of the three cinemas - the new Gaiety, the old Savoy, or the much older Kilgallon. All three sported posh tip-up seats – a facility unknown in our local hall in Manorhamilton that posed as a cinema once a week.

Half an hour before departure time, I boarded the Bus Éireann coach for Manorhamilton. From a rear seat I had a commanding view of the still-empty bus. As I sat waiting, a pleasant sense of homecoming took hold of me. The laid-back attitude and relaxed mood of arriving passengers was comforting. When I reflected on my earlier DART journey and the cultural and social contrast with my present surroundings I was ever so pleased to be home again.

The arrival of the bus-driver had an electrifying effect. His presence immediately induced an air of conviviality among the previously silent passengers. I was soon to discover that Padraig McKeon, the driver in question, was a man of no mean personality. As the journey progressed, the sense of harmony and rapport throughout the bus became, for me at any rate, something special, even inspiring. It was obvious that Padraig was considered something of an institution by my fellow travellers. He was on first-name terms with each passenger. It was refreshingly obvious that both travellers and driver had a very special relationship. This was not confined to good-humoured conversation, as I gleaned from Padraig's concern for the safety of an elderly passenger, when he left his seat and escorted her across the street in the midst of heavy traffic. Such willing assistance was tendered on every occasion, as passengers departed or joined us on our journey. Where in the world would one find such spontaneous care and concern on a public transport system? Thanks to Padraig, and despite the rush and bustle of modern times, much of the care and courtesy of other days still survived.

For the remainder of the journey my thoughts wandered and in imaginative expectation I visualised scenes from yesteryear. How much change had occurred over the years? Would I find anything to link with those memories which had somehow survived the passage of time? As the bus sped onwards through familiar countryside the hum of conversation prevailed, as Padraig affably engaged with all the passengers. It had all the trappings of a family outing. Again I could not but reflect on the character and mood of my surroundings and that earlier DART journey into Dublin.

The journey from Sligo took us through lovely Glencar, with its celebrated waterfall popularised by William Butler Yeats:

Where the wandering water gushes
From the hills above Glencar,
In pools among the rushes
That scarce could bathe a star[*]

I had travelled this road on Christmas Eve in 1941 with Matt, my young companion from Manorhamilton. We had cycled the sixteen miles to Sligo that morning. Our precise reason for going to Sligo is now vague but it had probably something to do with going to the pictures. More pertinent is my vision of the magical return journey through Glencar that evening. A heavy frost had fallen over the countryside, which was bathed in bright moonlight from a starry sky. It was a landscape dotted with traditional little farm houses. As we pedalled our way homewards on that Christmas Eve night a lighted candle burned in the window of every house. This was a widespread practice at the time; it symbolised a welcome to the Holy Family seeking shelter on the first Christmas Eve. That frosty night, a landscape dotted with candle-lit windows and the company of my youthful companion has become a treasured memory.

Now, as we journeyed onwards, I fell to musing on scenes from yesteryear and the memories I might revive of boyhood companions, youthful escapades, people and places. I would take a stroll through the familiar streets, visit old haunts, walk the river bank, tread on the disused railway track, or take a look at my old school. I was indeed

---

[*] William Butler Yeats "The Stolen Child"

becoming captivated!

While this musing over my visit was pleasant and evocative there were times when I inwardly deliberated within myself on the merits of nostalgia. There have been enormous changes in Ireland since my days in Manorhamilton and no doubt much of this change has been for the better. Most people have more money, are better educated and have greater opportunities in life. They have more freedom and there is no longer a fear of expressing one's opinion or of questioning matters.

This is not to say that we have arrived in Utopia – far from it indeed. We have greater purchasing power than ever before. With this increased affluence there are more cars, bigger and better roads and faster travel – yet hundreds die or are maimed in traffic accidents every year. Travel has become more frustrating and dangerous than ever before. Thankfully, new and better houses are built all over the country, yet villages become dormer settlements for larger towns, and communities suffer. Tax incentives encourage the building of holiday homes that are frequently occupied for only two weeks in the year – yet many are unoccupied. The compensation mentality thrives and there is now a rush to litigation on the slightest pretext. Society has become greedy, vulgar and materialistic. Standards of behaviour, unacceptable in the recent past, are now commonplace. The ethical standards in business, politics, public affairs and moral issues are frequently regarded as of little or no consequence. Time is the currency of the day and must be paid for. Voluntary work is left to the few. A sense of public service or social obligation is regarded as 'old hat' and not for the ambitious.

Of course it is popular to deride the past, as it makes the present look better than it really is. Avoiding this cynical attitude, I cling to the belief that returning to our past is a wonderful experience. A little more respect for the past might help us to manage the present and future a little better. In the past I might sense the touch of a vanished hand, the words of a forgotten song, take a walk with old pals, re-live in an old house, listen to an old record, experience old loyalties, or even play a game of football again. As the man said, 'the past is another country...' I don't mind going there from time to time – that is not to say that the past was all beautiful! However, a touch of reality in any assessment of present times can benefit from a little reflection on the past.

We cannot forget that our true roots spring from the natural world around us: the hedgerows, rivers, fields, mountains and lakes, the birds of the air – in short, from an all powerful nature.

Meanwhile, as we continued our journey and my fellow passengers gradually dispersed one by one as they reached their destinations, there were personal farewell greetings from Padraig to each one as they alighted from the bus. "Good luck with the hay." "See you next week." "Don't forget that bag," and so on. The spontaneous chat and farewell greetings were confirmation of a long-established affinity between passengers and trusted driver.

For the latter part of the journey, I continued to enjoy the scenery – the high road and the low road – the twisty road – the waterfall – the valley that lay smiling before me – the blue smoke from the few remaining little farm houses that curled upwards to the evening sky – the peace and tranquillity that prevailed. As we approached our destination and the familiar scene unfolded my thoughts were of tomorrow and a rekindling of faded memories. Where would I stay and who would I meet? Would anybody remember me? What might I find during my visit?

Chapter 7

First Day in Town

My bed and breakfast accommodation was an old Victorian house in the heart of the town. It had been a small private hotel during my youth and I was happy that it had not been distastefully updated. Next morning I awoke to the sound of twittering finches and chattering sparrows near my window. When I opened the faded lace curtains the large bedroom flooded with morning sunshine and I felt a surge of delight as the never-forgotten view unfolded before me. It was as if Benbo Mountain had been patiently waiting to greet me and that I had suddenly met up again with a long lost friend.

In Manorhamilton there is no escaping Benbo. Its shape and size dominates the surrounding landscape. Throughout my youthful years I was ever-conscious of its imposing position on the edge of the town, and, as I had so often observed, the fleeting clouds were still weaving that magic patchwork of colour and shadow across its ancient face.

Those reflections on Benbo Mountain stirred emotional thoughts of times long past: of a world in the aftermath of the Great War, of a land still blighted by the trauma of civil war and the economic hardships imposed by the Second World War. My boyhood belonged to those in-between years as the potent events of the late 1930s shaped for ever the destiny of our young generation. But now it was time to have breakfast and afterwards to take a walk in search of memories.

The little town of Manorhamilton, in North Leitrim, lies about half-way between the larger towns of Enniskillen and Sligo. It is surrounded by peaceful glens and silent mountains, and is a friendly little place where history and tradition run deep. This is a town of two traditions - that of the O'Rourkes of Breffni, and the planter-followers of Sir Frederick Hamilton. Here are the ivy-clad ruins of Hamilton's castle and a picturesque old church perched high on an ancient fortress, both of which have dominated a scene little changed for centuries. Here also, are the last vestiges of an old Union Workhouse, and a sad memorial to a victim of the tragic civil war. The town retains a few crumbled walls of a "Big House", once the home of a prominent gentry family, and the remains of an extinct railway line which once linked North and South. Each of these things forms a silent witness from the not-too-distant past.

On this first morning of my visit I took a leisurely walk to the Bee Park in the center of town. I was drawn there by recollections of carefree days and evenings spent within its confines. For many of us, football was the passion in life, and it was here that great dreams were dreamt and youthful imagination took full flight. Often the long shades of evening yielded to darkness as, reluctantly, we trudged our homeward way arguing over our most recent contest. Tread gently on my reservoir of dreams!

Those years of my growing up in Manorhamilton were a time of economic depression; there was little scope for anything other than the most elementary recreational facilities. There was no school sports field, playground, swimming pool or any other amenities that are now common. Having such basic requirements as a set of football jerseys, or indeed even a football, depended entirely on voluntary local efforts such as selling raffle tickets, or other forms of fund-raising. In hindsight, I feel indebted to those dedicated individuals who gave of their time to running local football clubs, boy scout groups, and such organisations. They gave leadership and encouragement during our crucial adolescent years.

Although Bee Park was the Mecca for most of our sporting activities it was sometimes forsaken for the adjoining lands of Skreeny, which were a blessing to the town. Here both young and old walked and played unhindered by the Land Commission fences that were to follow. A few moss-shrouded stones are all that now remain of the impressive Skreeny House, once the seat of the Cullen family who had lived there for almost two-hundred years during the eighteenth and nineteenth centuries. The Cullens were benevolent landlords who contributed significantly to the life of the town. Later in life, I learned of Skreeny's history and I realised how little I had then known of the place.

As I wandered through Bee Park, overlooked by the towering presence of Benbo Mountain and the nearby ruins of Hamilton's Castle, my musings on Skreeny were sidetracked by thoughts of Castle Street. It always seemed as if it were a place apart because of its characters, its village pump, and the games we played within the shadow of the old Castle ruins. My playmates there had an intense loyalty to that part of the town. It was almost as if it was another country – the Republic of Castle Street. Certainly, there were times when those of us who came from other parts of the town were made very aware of the *importance* of Castle Street by its young inhabitants. Perhaps it was the history of the place. After all, Sir Frederick Hamilton had been the founder and "the boss" all those years ago. Descendants or not, I always thought that my pals were very proud of their inheritance – whether in the local street games or in pursuing their own particular enterprises. As was indeed appropriate the bridge at Castle Street was a clear and definitive point of reference. Whenever I crossed that bridge it was like entering a new country – and I might require the approval and goodwill of some of my peers. Perhaps even a passport. For all that, some of my best and dearest childhood pals were 'Castle Street men' – even if they did insist on naming the only band in town *The Castle Street Band.*

One of the more colourful characters comes to mind. Peter was a tombstone sculptor and occupied one of the street's aesthetic little cut-stone houses overlooked by the nearby impressive ruins of Hamilton's Castle. I say *occupied* rather than *lived in,* because Peter had his own lifestyle. He carried on his monumental stone-cutting in the centre of the kitchen, all the windows of which remained broken for as long as I could remember. I presume that he slept upstairs, but certainly his domestic arrangements seemed very unusual. Peter was unmarried and seldom cared too much about the niceties of dress or the use of a razor. It was not as if he was cultivating a beard – just that he rarely shaved. My abiding vision of this stone-cutter is of a very big, strong man, dressed in baggy trousers and hob-nailed boots, chipping away at huge lumps of granite on his kitchen floor, while he freely chatted and entertained any young boys who might care to keep him company.

Now, Peter was not particularly disposed toward religious practise and we understood that he seldom went to Mass. In those days this was unheard-of and young boys were agog at the thought of anyone behaving in such a manner. This created an aura around Peter that in our young minds enhanced his hard-man status. I am sure, though, that his public image was of little concern to him.

It so happened that Peter found himself a patient in the local hospital which was run by an order of nuns. In bed one morning he was delighted to see that, surprisingly and unusually, he had been given egg and toast for breakfast.

As he was about to eat his egg the good nun rushed into the ward and excitedly snatched the tray away, crying out; "That's not for you, but for Mr. Brady"

Left speechless and with the egg-top balanced precariously on his spoon, Peter proclaimed in a loud voice, "They say that for every woman there was a man made, but the man that missed you had God's blessing!"

That was Peter!

I thought of the old village pump on Castle Street. Local history records that in the 1800s plans to erect this pump were debated in the British House of Commons. It so happened that a friend of mine successfully rescued the old village pump from obscurity long after it had fallen into disuse, and it now adorns a pleasant front garden in the Dublin Suburbs.

Old village pumps had an important role in community life throughout Ireland and the provision of water on tap in the village street was seen as a huge leap forward. There was also a certain social spin-off from the village pump. It was a meeting place where all who came with buckets and pails spread the news, and gossiped too. Going to the village pump was not regarded as a chore in an era devoid of radio or television, and other amenities now so much taken for granted. Indeed, 'village pump politics' was a staple element of village life.

Generations come, generations go,
And you stood firm, it seemed for ever;
Sphinx-like on your granite plinth,
Purveyor for all who choose to drink.

Rugged youths and scampering lads
Came thirsting to your spout,
As panting dogs from down the street,
Parched tongues sated at your feet.

While comely maids and busy mums,
Sometimes one, sometimes two,
With pails and cans to fill,
Lingered patiently on your arm,

And when your time had come,
A thoughtful heart and helpful hands,
Sped you away from Cluainin to Clonkeen.

There now you rest,
By flowered walk and velvet lawn,
Newly painted, quite serene,
Reflecting thoughts for those who dream.

As I left my beloved Bee Park, my steps took me along Main Street where I recalled the days of going to the pictures in Connolly's Hall. Entry to the hall was via a short narrow laneway and a steep wooden stairway. It was constructed of timber and asbestos and there were no fire escapes or anything in the nature of emergency exits. But 'you paid your money and took your chance.' On entry, usually well before commencement time, one had the unique experience of 'walking the plank' so to speak As the projector and the screen were, for some unexplained reason, positioned the wrong way around, you were obliged, on entering, to face those already seated and to walk the length of the hall to obtain a seat.

As there was only one projector, a break in projection was necessary after each reel. These intervals usually lasted about ten minutes and were regarded as an opportunity to light up and have a smoke or engage in conversation. Nobody ever complained about these shortcomings and indeed, it has to be said, there was uniqueness about the event. 'Going to the pictures' in Connolly's Hall was, for many, as much a social occasion as a cine-enthusiast's outing.

Now Manorhamilton is a hilly little town and, on reaching the crest of Boley Hill, I paused for breath and gazed at the scene before me. It was Our Lady's County Hospital where once stood what was called the County Home, or Union Workhouse. I happily surrendered to the urge to revisit, at least in memory, those scenes of boyhood years, which I had spent within the confines of that old place.

It consisted of an assembly of old buildings, surrounded by tall trees which were home to a large rookery of crows and jackdaws. As I looked back, the scenes came tumbling into my imagination; I heard the distant sounds of the old rookery as if they were beckoning me home from school. It must have been around 1930 when I first became aware of the squabbling crows, which had long before then become sitting tenants in the lofty tree tops. As a young boy, short-cutting my way to school, those penthouse tenants were an endless source of fascination. I watched the springtime scenes of nest-building, and the evening spectacle of homing birds, which terminated only when the last roosting place had been occupied. Such were the simple pleasures of those boyhood years. The old workhouse, the trees and the crows were inseparable.

It was in the year 1928 that I first came to live in the County Home in this small market town in North Leitrim. I was five years of age at the time and my mother, who was Assistant Matron at the County Home, was taking me there to live with her. We had travelled from Pomeroy in Co. Tyrone. Our journey that autumn day was on the Great Northern Railway (GNR) to Enniskillen and from there on the less-known Sligo Leitrim & Northern Counties Railway (SL&NCR). Both railways have long since been consigned to the dustbin of railway history.

On that first trip to Manorhamilton, the evening train steamed and puffed at the approaches to the station, then slowed and chugged its way along the banks of the Owenmore River. It was here that I caught my first glimpse of what was known to many as the 'Workhouse,' buildings, silhouetted high on a hillside. Little did I then realise that this old place would become my home and playground for the happy years that followed. One of my abiding recollections is the short journey from the railway station to the County Home. It was a journey I would travel many times during those ensuing carefree years.

For now, I was content to once again mount my mental bicycle and, in my imagination, to cycle along on a fine summer afternoon from that old railway station, past an abandoned thatched cottage, over the Curley Bridge, and down a little cart-track to an old sawmill, that was once a corn-mill. Then, back again by the banks of the quietly-flowing Owenmore River, which echoed the cries of youths at play, the drone of insects, the distant sounds of barking dogs and lowing cattle. It was at that time the haunt of fishermen and boys with homemade river rafts. I remember the dusty, silent, road where scented hawthorn sweetened the boundary walls of the County Home. There a rustic entrance of crumbling stone and ageing iron gates which led through the shade of lofty trees, past boxwood borders to well-trodden steps and up to the weathered doorway. I was a passive witness to the last years in the life of an old building that for nearly one hundred years had been the purveyor of both pain and healing to impoverished generations seeking refuge from famine, poverty and destitution.

I sometimes accompanied my mother as her made her daily matron's rounds. A visit to the storeroom upstairs was always an exciting experience for me. It was stacked with all sorts of supplies required for the day-to-day management of the Home; I thought it a sort of Aladdin's Cave. Here a gleaming assortment of new buckets, spades, forks, tin basins and a varied selection of hardware dangled from the high ceiling. Shelves stacked high with new linen sheets, bedspreads, pillows and mattresses lined the whitewashed walls. A variety of boxes full of nails, wax, polishes, threads and leather for repairing shoes were stacked in orderly file. But best of all were the coils of 'pig-tail' plug tobacco, from which a weekly supply was cut and distributed to the male inmates. To me that remote little storeroom was a magic place.

As the mood took me, I often meandered through the male wards and exchanged a boyish greeting with a few of the more enlightened inmates. Paddy McSharry was my favourite. Paddy had a deformed leg and moved with great difficulty on wooden crutches. He had lived for many years on a small farm near Glenfarne until his wife died. Having no close relatives, he was unable to manage his little farm and was obliged to seek care in the County Home. He was one of the few who always wore his own suit, and this set him aside as a man apart from the others.

I always looked forward to meeting Paddy, and frequently wandered into the ward where he slept with about ten others. As I perched myself at the foot of his bed and engaged in boyish chat, a sense of warmth and friendship prevailed. Although well advanced in years, he always seemed to lend an attentive and encouraging ear to my childish fantasies. When the opportunity arose, I sometimes 'nicked' a slice of tobacco for Paddy on those visits to the stores. Perhaps it was the absence of my father, who died when I was eleven months old, but, whatever the reason, the chemistry ran high between us.

The white bedspreads, the air smelling of burning turf, strong tobacco, carbolic disinfectant and the open turf fire, were abiding memories of my visits to Paddy. Some years later, after the place had been closed down and the inmates transferred to Carrick-on-Shannon, I recall my sadness on being told that Paddy, my kindly friend, had died. He had been very special to my young life and even now, some seventy years later these recollections of Paddy stir tender emotions of what might otherwise seem an irrelevant episode.

During those early years of growing up in this unusual setting, we were content to pursue our interests within the confines of our immediate surroundings. We had no reason, other than going to school, to visit the town. A few hilly fields known as 'the farm' behind the County Home were bordered by the nearby Owenmore River. In the lush green meadows by the river bank we enjoyed our simple pastimes in the seemingly never-ending days of summer. No talk then of polluted waters, global warming or the need for carbon credits!

When the doors of the County Home closed for the last time in 1936, it was time to move on. But the ambience of that unique place still lingers, as passing years sow the seeds of recollection and the swift sands of the hourglass run out.

Chapter 8

My School and Boyhood Haunts

I was so captivated by my reminiscences that I decided to spend another day along the banks of the Owenmore River, where grassy banks and deep brown pools had been host to the boyish episodes of my growing years. To my delight, I came upon the ruins of an old sawmill and the remains of its huge wooden waterwheel which had fascinated me all those years ago. There were other footprints in the sands of time: the bend in the river were we gathered on summer days, well-worn stepping stones to popular fishing pools and short-cuts taken to avoid difficult terrain.

A river, large or small, enhances any town, and this attractive little town is fortunate in that it has not one, but three rivers. While not major waterways, they are typical of the many little rivers, which grace the towns and countryside of Ireland. The Owenmore, and its sister river, the smaller Owenbeg, circle the town in an East-West pincher movement, before joining the larger river Bonet on its way to Sligo. A calm, deep bend in the gently flowing Owenmore, not far from the old railway track on the outskirts of the town, was the setting for our favourite swimming pool. Known locally as Parkes's Hole, it was the scene of many pleasant escapades. On sunny Sunday afternoons young boys and men crowded the grassy riverbank in happy camaraderie. Stories were told, songs were sung, and innocent games were played. The sun always seemed to shine in those days.

The SL&NCR ran close to the river. The sound of the puffing engine, belching clouds of steam and smoke, heralded the train's approach long before it came into view from the riverbank, as we rushed to the best vantage point. From there, as the smell of smoke hung heavy, each passing train was greeted with lusty cheers and frantic handwaving until it was lost to view. Indeed, it was normal practice in those days of innocent distraction to wave a friendly greeting to passing trains. It was a welcome and God-speed-you-on-your-way kind of greeting, and was invariably reciprocated by passengers - especially those on the Sunday excursions.

A favourite pastime was to identify the trains by their colourful names. These were: *Fermanagh, Leitrim, Lurganboy, Lissadell, Hazlewood, Lough Melvin, Sir Henry, Enniskillen, Lough Gill, and Lough Erne.* The Railway Company chose the names, as they had strong associations with the railway's history, and they were proudly displayed on a handsome decorative nameplate on the side of the engine. The colour of the coaches was unlined maroon, while the engines were painted a lined olive green, or a plain black. First opened in 1879, this little railway ran the 48 miles between Enniskillen and Sligo, until its closure in 1957. Construction commenced in 1877 and progressed by stages until it connected with the Midland Great Western Railway (MGWR) line at Collooney on the 7th November 1887.[*] It was a unique railway, boasting a modest total of seven steam engines at the end of its life. That the SL&NCR was unique in many respects may be gleaned from the words of railway historian H. C. Casserly: "The Sligo Leitrim & Northern Counties Railway was a highly individual line. There was nothing quite like it, even in Ireland, and, unfortunately, there never can be again."[†]

Also worth mentioning was the interesting position of the little station at Belcoo in County Fermanagh, about ten miles from Manorhamilton. Officially known as Belcoo & Blacklion station, it was probably the most unusual railway station in Europe – if not in the world. Following the partition of Ireland in 1922, the border ran through the closely adjoining villages of Belcoo, Co. Fermanagh, Northern

---

[*] Neil Whitby Spinks, "The Sligo, Leitrim and Northern Counties Railway" *An Irish Railway Pictorial.* (c) 2001

[†] H. C. Casserley, *Irish Railways in the Heyday of Steam.*

Ireland, and Blacklion, Co. Cavan in the Irish Free State - now the Republic of Ireland. The station at Belcoo, therefore, served two separate political jurisdictions. Although it had become the final crossing point on an international frontier, it never quite attained the importance of Berlin's Checkpoint Charlie.

This little railway was hugely important to the local community. Manorhamilton was the engineering centre of the SL&NCR, with locomotive, carriage and wagon shops, which employed upwards of one hundred local men. Its closure was a turning point in the economic and social life of the town. For many it was a turning point along life's uncertain path.

But let us return to the gently flowing Owenmore River. High on a hill, overlooking those riverside scenes of joyful activity, the old Union Workhouse had silently surveyed the landscape since 1842, but, for now, suffice it to say that its raison d'être never troubled our young minds – we had other pleasures to pursue.

The Curley Bridge over the Owenmore, not far away, on the outskirts of the town, offered deep fishing pools for salmon and trout, as well as the pleasure of navigating our homemade river-rafts. These were constructed from old planks and empty tar-barrels, which we somehow managed to ingeniously scavenge from an unsuspecting source. Although the Owenmore is not quite the Mississippi, reaching the far side in our home-built version of Tom Sawyer's raft was considered a major triumph – as a premature sinking was usually the most likely outcome.

Fishing for eels on summer evenings from the parapet of the bridge was a pastime which often took our fancy as the mood inspired. It was inexpensive, requiring only a home-made fishing rod, strong fishing-line and eel-hook which could be purchased at four for a penny. A cork wrapped in silver paper was the only optional extra required. Large black-headed worms from a local dung-heap served as bait. Late evening, around 10.00 pm, was always the best time, and as the evening shadows fell the silver-wrapped cork would, hopefully, send clear signals to the eager and excitable young anglers perched high overhead. As weather dictated, we became anglers, cowboys, sailors or soldiers along the banks of this delightful little river

Close to the bridge, a sawmill was approached by a pleasant little cart track along the riverbank, past deep river bends overhung with leafy shade. The well-worn cart track to the mill provided easy access to popular fishing pools. The bushes were host to precious fly-life and home to the blackbird, thrush, and all kinds of chattering bird-life. The flowing waters had been harnessed many years before by means of a huge waterwheel as a source of energy for an old corn-mill. In my boyhood days it was no longer a corn mill, having been converted to a sawmill. The large wooden waterwheel, slowly rotated by the flow of diverted river water, was connected to a huge circular saw, which greedily sliced the largest trees. Here, to our youthful delight, the buzzing saw fused with the sounds of the flowing river, and the smell of fresh sawdust from the freshly felled trees added sweet fragrance to nature's other blessings. The buzz and activity of the mill, with its huge waterwheel, was music to our young ears. Here indeed we found adventures far beyond the reach of Huckleberry Finn or Tom Sawyer.

Further down-stream was a small hydropower-station that generated electricity for the town. It, too, like the sawmill, drew its energy from the Owenmore via a series of ramparts, millraces and sluice-gates. This little 'electric mill', as it was popularly known, was a private local enterprise until taken over by the ESB (Electricity Supply Board) in the 1950s. For most of its lifetime the hydropower station was in the hands of a workforce of only two men - Michael Meehan and Willie 'Bunter' D'Arcy.

Not only did these men staff and maintain the mill, year in, year out – day and night – but they were also at the beck and call of the entire town for most of their working lives. Bunter, noted for his expertise as an angler, could justifiably be described as "Lord Owenmore," such was his knowledge of every twist and turn in the river. As we gathered and strove vainly for success with rod and line at our favourite pools, Bunter often descended upon us. Flashing and casting with apparent ease, he had no difficulty in plucking a silver trout from under our noses. Then as quickly as he had arrived, he passed silently on his way along the riverbank, leaving us lesser mortals in open-mouthed amazement. How did he do it? We never found the answer. I'm told that his beloved green-heart fishing rods accompanied Bunter to his final resting place.

But times had changed and only faint traces of the old mills now remain. Sadly, the scene has become overgrown and derelict. Litter and waste have stretched their ugly tentacles across the once-clear waters of our beloved Owenmore. Who knows, perhaps those who once graced its green grassy banks, toiled in the little mills, or fished and sported in its magic waters, still haunt this delightful place?

The Owenmore wound its way past the boys' school on the outskirts of the town. Built in 1842, the school was of the same vintage as the Union Workhouse, later to be the County Home. Through those formative years we made the daily trek through the front grounds of the County Home, under evergreen trees and over a crumbling stone wall to school in Ross Lane. At about 9 o'clock each morning we reached the crest of Boley Hill, where usually Bob McNabb's oil tanker was spurting blue exhaust smoke in preparation for the day's deliveries.

It was a common sight to see two men seated in the roadside ditch breaking stones by hand with a stone hammer. They were in the ditch as we passed in the morning and still there when we were returning late in the afternoon. Stone-breaking was one thing in fine weather, but quite another on cold, wet Leitrim days. Road maintenance was archaic in those days and a tarred surface was the exception rather than the rule. Such were the means by which the County Council gave local employment and acquired material for repairing the roads during those difficult economic times.

The hedges along that road to school carry abiding recollections which were close to this young boy's heart. There was the springtime growth of fresh green shoots, the bursting forth of white blossoms and the sweet smell of the scented hawthorn. And then, seemingly in no time at all, the red winter berries arrived. The cycle of nature had been completed, marking the passing of the year as we made that daily trek to school.

On rare occasions when the school failed to open, because of flu or some other reason, we were given a holiday. This welcome and unexpected good news was always greeted with lusty cheering and flinging of school bags in the air. That regular homeward path from school was sometimes forsaken for a more adventurous course along the river banks, through the electric mill that supplied electricity to the town. Here the hum of machinery, the smell of oil, and the vibrant sounds of a river, harnessed by ramparts, sluices and locks, fascinated and challenged the young adventurer.

From my school hundreds of boys from the town and surrounding districts took their first hesitant step on the road of life. Memories still burn brightly of rain-filled days, when we stood by the classroom wall and peered through foggy windows for the tell-tale silver stream on the face of Benbo Mountain which foretold a full brown flood in the river below. And so, as the morning passed, our impatience grew for the closing hour and a homeward dash for rod and line and a place on the river bank. There was no school sports field in those days. We created our own improvised pastimes, such as lunch-time ball games in Ross Lane or football on the Commons, as we made our way home from school.

Our first years were in the junior school with Mrs. McGrath. Later we moved upstairs to Mr. McGrath for the remainder of our time there. The classroom comprised of the entire upstairs floor. It was spacious, and to say that it was 'airy' is certainly an understatement. It was a very old building with draughty windows, bare wooden floors and a high ceiling. A fireplace with an open grate at one end was the only source of heating. Boys from the 'country' gave a cart load of turf each year and those from town contributed five shillings towards the cost of heating. Maps of Ireland, the British Isles, the Dominions (coloured red), Europe and the rest of the world, adorned the whitewashed walls. The classroom furniture was basic and meagre. It consisted of rows of long wooden desks that seated five or six pupils, a wag-on-the-wall clock, the teacher's desk and a chair. Each morning, one of us was directed to refill the little ink-wells in every desk. Roll-call was at 9 o'clock each morning and each one present answered *anseo* (here) when their name was called out by the teacher. The total number present, which sometimes exceeded one hundred, was then marked with chalk on a small blackboard.

Now if those stones could only talk, the walls of this seat of learning would surely echo poignant memories of those morning treks to school. Most mornings a 'certain crowd' gathered in the doorway of Wilson's corner shop in the centre of town before continuing the journey to school. Here we awaited the last stragglers to join our tardy band. Only when a sufficient number had congregated did we decide to move on and complete the journey to school. In a slow procession we made our belated way to school, and a confrontation with an angry schoolmaster. Having clambered up the stone steps, we fearfully hesitated in the inner porch before mustering courage for the final dash. Then, one by one, we ran the gauntlet past the Master who awaited us inside with his long and ready cane. With hand tucked in sleeve and arm held high for protection, we dashed through the open doorway in the hope of avoiding whatever punishment he might inflict. The Master hit at legs, arms or wherever he could land a blow. But it was a very brief encounter, as, once you passed his lashing cane, he turned his angry attention for the next offender who, if smart enough, had already made his hurried dash to safety. It was part of the morning routine – school would not have been the same without our beloved, well respected, Master McGrath and those morning confrontations.

Chapter 9

Family Connections

After breakfast on my third morning, I took a leisurely stroll downtown. The familiar streets were enveloped in warm sunshine and little had changed over the years. For one brief moment it seemed as if I might meet an old friend or somebody who might recognise me, but the passage of time had wreaked havoc!

The small grocery shop that was once the town's post office evoked thoughts of other days. Like all small town post offices in was not just a place for posting letters – it was the town's communications centre. There were no evening deliveries, and it was common practise to call in person and collect your letters. People met and there was time for a chat – not unlike going to the village pump. The post office was also the local telephone exchange, and no doubt the post mistress was privy to much of the goings-on in Manorhamilton.

Long before the advent of mobile phones, the delivery of telegrams was an important service provided by the post office. In the cities and large towns telegraph boys were permanently employed, but in small towns and villages the delivery of telegrams depended on some local young lad with a bicycle. Telegrams were used only for news of an urgent or important nature – such as a death or serious illness. However, with the coming of the Irish Hospital Sweepstakes a new dimension was given to the little green envelope containing a telegram. The lucky winners of large prizes were immediately notified by telegram. And so, the green telegram envelope was indicative of good or bad news, of great consequence.

On one occasion the post-mistress invited me to deliver a telegram to a household about four miles from town. Of course, I had no idea of the contents of the telegram. The recipient could have drawn a horse in the

Sweepstake for all I knew or cared, but I jumped at the possibility of making some pocket money. I recall that my remuneration for this assignment was sixpence (now about two cents) and that I punctured my bike on the stony, mountain road. Not one of my most profitable enterprises, I'm afraid.

Across the street from the shop that was at that time the post office, stands a memorial cross to Phil Gilgunn, a relative of mine from nearby Ballyboy who was an IRA leader in the War of Independence. The memorial marks the spot where he was shot dead during the Civil War in 1922. The memorial had been erected there when I was about seven years old, and I know little of the circumstances surrounding his death. However, I well recall the many times I passed this spot on my way to the nearby Bee Park without thought or care. I was more focused on football than the tragedies of the Civil War.

My father, who came from Holy Well, Belcoo, and Phil Gilgunn were cousins and, as was so often the case, they held different political views on the Treaty of 1921 that brought the Irish Free State into existence. They died within two years of each other.

It was only in later years that I came to fully appreciate the trauma and sorrow then visited on both households. I paused to take a photograph of this image from the past and I thought of the political turmoil of those times, of the divided loyalties brought about by the Civil War, of my father's work for Michael Collins, of his first cousin Phil Gilgunn – who took the republican side and frequently sought shelter and safety at Ora, and of their premature deaths in 1922 and 1924. As the years roll by, I sometimes reflect on how different life might have been if the events of those years had been otherwise.

My thoughts drifted to happy days spent at my father's home near Holy Well. It was a typical small Irish farmhouse, high up in the mountain townland of Oramore. We always referred to it as Ora. Following my father's death in 1924, my mother, who had settled in Manorhamilton, maintained close contact with her in-laws in Ora. It was a short rail journey on the SL&NCR to Belcoo where my Uncle Hugh would meet us at the little railway station with pony and trap and take us the two miles to Ora.

I recall my excitement as the little pony slowly climbed the narrow hilly road and the beautiful landscape unfolded. The wide expanse of Lough McNean, with its little islands shimmering below us in those hazy summer days, is a scene embedded in my memory.

The Gilgunn connection with Ora stretched back to the 18th century, and my boyhood visits there in the 1930s were in the twilight years of the family's presence in that beautiful but difficult mountain country. The ensuing years would see the dispersal of families, the gradual disappearance of homesteads and their inevitable surrender to conifer trees.

It was a winding, hilly climb to the house that was located at the highest point in a rugged landscape. I recall my boyish excitement when we finally arrived in the cosy, warm kitchen to be greeted by grandfather and aunties. From those fleeting days linger visions of happy hours spent within the bosom of a caring and loving household.

The long, low building with its tidy thatched roof and gleaming white walls was typical of most homesteads of that era and was a replica of the Gilgunn home at Ballyboy. Gloriously located on such a high plateau, it commanded a wonderful panoramic view of the entire length of Loch McNean and as far as the mountains of Cavan and Leitrim. On a very fine evening even the Atlantic could be glimpsed at far away Bundoran in Co. Donegal. It was, indeed, a wide and varied landscape that stirred the mind and offered endless scope to my youthful imagination. Our immediate surroundings of little trout streams, bilberry bushes, rabbits and hares, colourful mountain heather, and the music of ascending larks, were for ever enhanced by a panoramic background of hills, lakes and tiny islands.

The moorlands behind the house were less favoured, except on those occasions when I went with Uncle Hugh or Aunt Nora to bring home the cows. It was late in the evening, the sun had long set behind the distant hills in the west and a chilly breeze ruffled the *ceannabhan* (bog cotton) as we strode in search of wayward cattle. But I was happy in Aunt Nora's company and comforted myself with thoughts of the homely kitchen that awaited our return, the warmth and comfort of the fireside, the open hearth, the singing kettle, the wide chimney – with views of starry skies for those who choose to look, the homely smell of burning turf, and the cosy little fireside and purring cat.

I remember one sultry August evening in 1930. The weather had been fine and warm for weeks. There were now signs of a break in the weather, and there had been faint rumbles of thunder in the far-away Leitrim hills earlier in the day. The last haycock had been 'dressed' before darkness fell and we made our way to the house satisfied that the day's work was done.

It was time for supper, and Aunt Nora served bowls of freshly-made porridge as we sat in a semi-circle around the kitchen fire. There was the usual chat about the weather and the satisfaction of having saved the last of the hay. It would soon be time to say the Rosary. Then suddenly without warning, a loud peal of thunder crashed overhead, shattering the peace of the little gathering. It was to be the first of many frightening peals in a night long to be remembered as the most violent thunder-storm in many years. The prayers were fervently offered as the thunder crashed over the isolated little farmhouse and its fearful occupants. I sat close to my Uncle Hugh, feeling sheltered and protected in his strong brown arms, yet terrified by the lightening outside as it flashed insistently under the kitchen door, until Aunt Nora covered the gap with some old sacking. At about 3am the storm abated and we thought it was all over.

Aunt Nora decided to make some tea and to relieve the tension by playing some gramophone records. Her second choice of record had just commenced when the house was suddenly shaken by a devastating clap of thunder. The storm returned with a vengeance. Uncle Hugh and Aunt Nora took turns at visiting the cow byre to pacify the frightened animals. Then the rains came and by day-break the storm was over, but it had been a long night of fear and apprehension in that little farmhouse, so remote and isolated in the high country of Fermanagh. The next day the countryside glistened from the effects of the heavy over-night rain and the warm hazy weather returned.

Whenever I visited Ora, the sight of my father's fishing rod hanging on the blackened kitchen rafters invariably sparked romantic thoughts in my young mind. At times I visualised an admiring dad and adoring son treading their heathery domain on some fishing expedition. About seven years had elapsed since his untimely death, when I was thrilled as Uncle Hugh, entrusted me for the first time with the beloved fishing rod. He had decided that we should go fishing in one of the many small lakes around Ora. My excitement new no bounds as I took the rod in my hands, and we made our way down the rocky *boreens* that led to Lough Hamill. My mother had often told me of my father's fondness for this little wayside lake and recalled how he had expressed a wish to pay a last visit there shortly before he died.

The occasion of that fishing expedition remains memorable to me for the peaceful setting – the babbling water lapping the shoreline, the tiny water fowl sheltering in the tall reeds, the calls of wild duck, mountain sheep, and a lonesome curlew. These serene surroundings were disturbed only by the excited cries of the young boy retrieving his first silver catch from the purple heather behind him.

Lough Ora, another small lake on the other side of the house, was noted for its plentiful brown trout. A quiet, peaceful place of bog, moorland and mountain streams, it was my father's favourite haunt. It seemed as if I was destined to retrace his footsteps, as I too became obsessed with the challenge of those elusive brown trout.

Now, my sojourn in my adopted home-town was coming to an end. As always, time was the enemy and, I had to move on.

Chapter 10

Further memories of Manorhamilton

It was to be the last day of my visit to the town where I had grown from childhood through boyhood into adolescence, and I was determined to make the most of it. At a time when the boom in house building, the increased density of traffic on the roads, and the expanding economy were changing the face of Ireland, my memories seemed more precious than ever.

What we used to call 'The Corner' was the junction of four streets which was a stopping place for those seeking a rendezvous with whoever might turn up. Although recollections of those years are quite diverse and relate to different areas of the town, the hub of life for me, and other teenagers, centred around this junction of Main Street, Tea Pot Lane, Sligo Road and New Line. The Corner was accepted as a natural meeting place where one might be lucky enough to meet with a favourite pal. Here, outside Rooney's Barber Shop or at Miss Cooney's Pub on the opposite side, you were usually assured of being able to chat with somebody you knew. Conversation would ensue, and depending on the time of year, the weather, the ages and dispositions of the participants, the course of the evening's activity was determined. This might be a trip to the nearby Bee Park for a game of football or the pursuit of some other favoured activity.

The Barber Shop was probably the favourite meeting place of all. There, at some time or other, Benny and Jimmy 'Midge' Rooney must have stroked the heads of nearly every man and boy in Manorhamilton. Saturday night was always the most crowded. Those were the days when many of the clients made a point of having themselves spick and span for Sunday – a case of 'Saturday splash for Sunday dash'. I have visions of Benny sharpening his cut-throat razor on the strong leather strop which hung near the window. We young lads were fascinated by his stance and rhythm as he stropped back and forth with his glistening steel blade. Benny was very fashion-conscious. He dressed in the latest style and we marvelled how his wide trouser legs at times completely covered his shiny patent leather shoes. This was surely something to be aspired to.

Of course, there are other memories. The Rooneys were very interested in soccer, and whenever we were disposed to playing that code the barber shop became an unofficial headquarters. A small back room off the shop served as a place where we gathered – sometimes two and sometimes more – to discuss the great plans we had for our youthful soccer team. Togs and jerseys were stored in biscuit tins. These we had purchased with the proceeds of one-penny raffle tickets which we sold with great gusto throughout the town. A book of 10 tickets could be purchased for the bargain price of six pence. I cannot recall the prizes offered, but it is safe to assume that few millionaires resulted. The trouble was that we never seemed to play any teams other than our own, as there were no other soccer teams in the area.

Manorhamilton in those days was one of those places where there was great rivalry between the GAA and soccer. Our young loyalties depended on the best deal on offer at the time, and sometimes on the attitudes of parents. Enticements to play a particular code could take the form of a new set of football jerseys or the promise of a high-profile unspecified fixture, but for sure neither Croke Park nor Old Tafford were ever on offer. I had little reason to be interested in Cooney's pub on the opposite corner. There Pat Cambell managed the pub on behalf of Miss Cooney. Pat, from Crossmaglen, was an enthusiastic GAA man who managed our minor football team of 1939-40. Across a little counter, just inside the front door, we spent many hours analysing the selection of teams and re-living games lost and won. In our beloved Bee Park, great dreams and young ambitions were given full rein as football became our passion in life. Often did the long shades of evening yield to darkness as reluctantly we trudged our homeward way arguing the merits of our recent combat.

When I returned, I noticed that the old milestone embedded against the corner of the pub was still there. It had been part of the streetscape for as long as I could remember. Data etched on the stone were removed in 1940 when Leitrim County Council carried out government instructions to have all visible road directions obliterated in anticipation of an enemy invasion. The German or Allied Forces were not to conveniently find their way if they arrived at Cooney's corner.

Nearby, a small unnamed residential laneway became known by the folksy name of Tea-Pot Lane. One morning in the late 1930s, to everyone's surprise, it was discovered that a home-made street nameplate bearing the patron saint's name had been erected on a gable-wall overnight. It seems that an enterprising citizen had decided to give the place a 'proper' name. Thus it was that St. Patrick's Terrace was born. I am not sure if the residents of Tea-Pot Lane where pleased or offended at this apparent threat to their inheritance.

Quickening my pace, to ensure that I would take in as much as possible, I made my way down to what had been Tea-Pot Lane and along the Commons, where I passed the ruins of the girls' school and recalled the day I sat there for my Primary School examination in 1937. It was one of those lovely June days, the sun shining brightly and the dew on the ground as I made my way to the examination hall full of hope and anxiety.

Further on, I came to the spot where one of my teenage pals had lived. The little thatched house of those days has long been demolished to make way for the all-devouring traffic. Matt belonged to a large family and worked in the local button factory. We struck up a happy relationship during our late teenage years. Without fail we made our weekly visits to the pictures in Connolly's Hall. I would call to the cottage home to find Matt preparing himself for the evening's entertainment, in shirt and trousers, washing and shaving from a tin basin perched on a three-legged stool in the middle of the kitchen floor. On his way home from his day's dusty work in the button factory, Matt would have purchased a Mac's Smile razor and a small bottle of hair oil. I was always somewhat amused at Matt's delicate stroke of the razor and the application of a goodly handful of hair-oil. All this took place while his lesser siblings went about their own business. Such were the times during those distant and somehow happy war years of the 1940s.

Bicycle rides to Kiltyclogher for the unveiling of the Sean McDermott memorial or cycling home from Sligo on Christmas Eve are but some of my fond memories of Matt. He was highly intelligent and, had he been given the opportunity, I am sure he would have made his mark in whatever calling he chose. Much to my surprise and sadness I learned one morning that he had gone to England. That was the last I ever heard of Matt.

All too quickly we moved on, fleet-footed, through adolescence into manhood. We were not to know it then but soon we would leave behind an easy-going life and a seemingly timeless place. In those days of exuberant youth, life would never end – or so we thought. But the winds of change and the tides of events were about to shape our future. The pack was being shuffled and life, like the river we knew so well, would follow its onward course. Some drew the long straw, others were less fortunate. Gathering war clouds soon released a torrent that changed and shortened the path of life for many. There remained but a few more years before the final uprooting in 1942. It was then that the little world I had known vanished for ever. With the departure of Matt and many others, life had changed. Suddenly I felt that I too had to go.

Down silent streets
Where old friends meet.
Muffled voices call.
To echo thoughts and dreams of days not yet beyond recall.

I continued on my ramble past the last faint traces of the long vanished County Home until I came to the stone bridge over the Owenmore River. My thoughts were now of days spent by the banks of this beautiful river and the many train journeys from the nearby railway station to Pomeroy in Co. Tyrone.

Chapter 11

A Sort of Homecoming

Next morning, as I lay in bed, my thoughts returned to Pomeroy. Although the railway was long gone, I considered the possibility of perhaps renting a car and making a fleeting visit there before returning to Dublin. Fortunately, I had made the acquaintance of the owner of the town's oldest garage whose grandfather had established the business there when I was a child. My sentimental revisiting had fostered a friendship between us and he readily placed a car at my disposal. And so it was that I took the road to Enniskillen after breakfast, and from there to Omagh and on to Pomeroy.

Midday clouds hung high over the Sperrin Mountains as I drove along the once-familiar winding road. I mused silently on life as the passing landscape unfolded its patchwork of green and gold with each familiar turn in the road. Infrequent visits over the years had kept alive memories of the village and its inhabitants, but, regrettably, the passing of time had brought about a natural wastage of friends from boyhood years. It had been ten years since my last visit there, and, even if it had been less, there would have been few who would have known me.

The unexpected sight of a police patrol, guns at the ready, in the nearby fields alerted me to the need for caution. Sadly, it seemed that the days were long gone when I could scamper carefree through the little roads and fields around the village. Faded election posters and graffiti, defiantly mocking the fluttering Union Jack high on the Protestant church, were reminders of an ancient and unresolved conflict. Nothing much had changed! And yet everything had changed!

The little village, swathed in afternoon sunshine, lazily stirred and roused itself for whatever business could be done, as silent houses and empty shops gazed at one another with vacant stare. The afternoon bus, with its three lonely passengers, spluttered hesitantly to a stop outside the small newsagent's shop on the deserted street.

I had in mind a brief walk through the village and the taking of some photographs to add to my store of memories. Tucked into a corner of The Diamond was a simple little single-storey house, whose long white walls reflected the warmth of the hazy afternoon sunshine. For me it had acquired, over the years, a deep emotional significance. It was my birthplace. It was in this little house that I had opened my eyes for the first time to the light of day.

Down the years, on those irregular and infrequent visits, it had become a significant stopover on my itinerary. It was always there, with its long, low white walls, nestling snugly into its corner of the village, unchanged and reassuring, and it never failed to stir memories of my earliest years. My widowed mother and I had left this house when I was only four years old, and there had never been a reason to return, as we had had no dealings with subsequent occupants. But I was always pleased that it was there when I did come back. I was happy that it survived with my memories. Such was its permanency in my affections that it would never have crossed my mind that some day it might cease to exist.

Now things seemed somehow different as I felt an unexplained sense of urgency — a last chance, not to be missed, of grasping a permanent memory of my old home. Perhaps I would never again return to the village, and I was determined to make the most of the opportunity. As I composed my picture carefully through the view-finder, I noticed that the hall-door was slightly ajar, and the once-white lace curtains were blowing through the half-open windows. Suddenly a thought struck me: could it be that the house was empty? With heart-throbbing anxiety I approached the half-open door. It yielded invitingly to my touch, and my pulse missed a beat as I realised that the house had been abandoned.

Stepping inside, I examined my deserted home, the torn and faded wallpaper, the broken table, a few upturned chairs, holy pictures, a torn mattress, and an assortment of household items scattered about the small rooms. My first reaction was one of revulsion at the desolate scene — the array of personal effects exposed to the world at large! Was this symptomatic of modern life — an unsavoury by-product of today's uncaring society?

> *Was there not a living relative or friend*
> *to come and blind the gaping public stare?*
> *Who would come and who could mend*
> *the lock and show some sign of care?*

When the first shock had passed, the full import of the scene burst upon me. I suddenly realised that it had been over sixty years since I had last stood, as a little four-year-old boy, within those self-same walls. I trembled in dread anticipation as my eyes slowly searched the small rooms — which uncannily appeared little changed — almost exactly as I would have envisaged them.

A deep silence prevailed throughout the little house, disturbed only by the rustle of the late autumn breeze through the riot of nettles, and the gentle tapping of an old wild-rose tree on the kitchen window. A shaft of evening sunlight pierced the gloom, and my thoughts drifted back those 60 years. Long-lost memories jockeyed for position, as I paused by the open-hearth fireplace where once old Granny aired my tiny clothes. Haunting visions competed for attention: a busy mother, a kindly neighbour calling, playing with cousins, the market-day haggling on the crowded Diamond, writing letters to Santa, Easter eggs, chatting with little companions, the sound of loving voices, whistling winds, attic mice at play, the scent of burning turf.

As emotive images formed I reluctantly — perhaps feeling cheated by fleeting time — stole a final all-embracing glance at my old home. I knew that never again would the vision return, and I was grateful for those brief but precious moments.

Once-white curtains blowing in the wind,
Wild roses knocking on a window pane,
Faded wallpaper and slanted holy picture,
Musty smell and ruptured mattress
Unlatched, weathered door and broken window-frame,
Poignant pointers all.
Drop the latch and turn away,
cherish memories of other days.

The fading daylight was casting shadows over the landscape as I set out on the return journey. Driving through the quiet countryside I reflected on the vagaries of life. My life had been a tale of three villages and a little town: the little village of Ringsend in Dublin's docklands, the old Viking village of Dalkey, and the mountain village of Pomeroy set high in the Sperrin Mountains, and the little town of Manorhamilton that nestles peacefully among the beautiful valleys of North Leitrim.

Chapter 12

Larkfield Days

An array of signposts to the past was now on my radar and I was so reluctant to leave Manorhamilton that I decided to indulge in another day of exploration and welcomed the opportunity for a stroll towards Larkfield where I had lived for those final adolescent years.

Passing the old St. Clare's Hall, now desolate and apparently abandoned, I thought of Father Jim who was the local curate for most of my young life in Manorhamilton. Small of stature, with quick step and fiery temper, he was a man not easily forgotten – at least not by some of the young boys who for one reason or another happened to fall within his orbit. My abiding impression of this priest conjures visions of a man in constant haste. In fact, he was renowned, and appreciated, for saying the late Mass in less than fifteen minutes.

Father Jim was a good pastoral priest who involved himself in the local community. As chaplain to our fledgling troop of boy scouts he was tutor, director, producer and casting director of the troop's first, and only, theatre venture – a Shakespearian drama no less.

With about four weeks preparation time, *Julius Caesar* would be staged in St. Clare's Hall on Easter Sunday night. I don't think the casting director relied very much on volunteers coming forward for the various character roles. Nomination was the name of the game! Father Jim nominated you for a part and that was all there was to it. You took the script home with you and God help those who had not learned their lines by the time of the next rehearsal.

Playing one of Shakespeare's Roman characters proved daunting enough, but, as there was not a cast of thousands to choose from it was necessary to play more than one role. The on-stage appearances of the young actors, in different roles with little or no change of costume would prove somewhat puzzling for a less than spellbound audience. But Father Jim was undaunted and pursued the dreaded weekly rehearsals to the limit. As I still retained my strong northern accent, I found myself frequently at the receiving end of his undoubted enthusiasm and blistering temper. His favourite critical outburst at my rendering of Shakespeare's lines was, "By God, they'll surely cheer for the Union Jack when they hear you!" But for all that, Father Jim was a decent, sincere man. When the concert was over and all the accolades paid he hurried to the dressing room in profuse appreciation. He heaped praise, sweets, and lemonade on each of his young charges – and cigarettes to those senior enough to accept.

As curate, Father Jim was of course subject to the authority of the Parish Priest. Now, the Monsignor was something of a godlike figure of much pomp and self-esteem. It so happened that a Guard of Honour was being provided by the troop for the funeral of a respected local dignitary. We were directed to assemble outside the church door and await the end of the funeral mass. Patience not being the strongest virtue of the young, an element of boredom arose, and spotting the loaded ripe plum trees in the Monsignor's nearby garden, three of us in a daredevil display of bravado decided to refresh ourselves for the forthcoming journey with a supply of the Monsignor's plums.

While it may not have been a repeat of the Garden of Eden, there was a sequel to what became known as the 'Boy Scouts and the Forbidden Fruit.' A few days after the funeral, Father Jim arrived at our school on Ross Lane and the three culprits were called forth. We were paraded from the classroom and marched across town by an irate curate to the large and uninviting Parochial House. Our apprehension was not lessened by perceptions of the Monsignor who was, in our young eyes, a very authoritarian figure. A tall, heavily built man, he projected an aura of importance and aloofness. We saw him as a person to be feared and one quite distant from our everyday lives and, in an era of omniscient church influence, his authority was certainly undisputed.

The newly-built handball alley adjacent to the parochial house was all the rage at the time. Evenings were given over to handball practice and the place would be crowded with onlookers. I still have visions of the Monsignor, in the full clerical regalia of the time, suddenly appearing through the small wicket-gate and strolling past the seated spectators as, caps in hand, they respectfully rose to their feet. And so we were brought before this mighty man who in stern voice admonished us on the gravity of our sin against the seventh commandment "Thou shall not steal." He did not know if we could ever obtain absolution and pondered the possibility of excommunication. In the event, no charges were preferred and the culprits, somehow, survived to tell the tale.

On reflection, I am of the opinion that Father Jim's short fuse had been ignited more as a result of having to comply with the Monsignor's orders than a sense of outrage at the loss of the precious plums. Such it seems was the lot of curates in the reign of 'Monsignor Plum'.

Noted for his no-frills approach to church duties, Father Jim never wasted time. He invariably took the late Mass on Sundays. However, his impatient urge to get on with the job could sometimes rebound on his innocent and unsuspecting parishioners. I recalled the occasion, on Good Friday, when I fell foul of his impatience. I was looking to my left while kneeling at the altar rails, waiting to kiss the crucifix being carried by the priest from the far end. Unfortunately, I did not realise that Father Jim was also bringing a crucifix from the opposite end. Suddenly without warning I received a bang on the head from Father Jim's brass crucifix. He was not a man to wait unnecessarily or to waste time on words if action brought results.

At that time, a story about Father Jim's call to visit a sick parishioner far up the mountain road at Tullyskeherny was doing the rounds. It was wintertime, very late at night, stormy and raining heavily as he set off on his visit. Not being quite familiar with the mountain terrain, he had great difficulty in locating the isolated farmhouse. Eventually, after much frustration, he came upon a house with a lighted window. Immediately, the door was opened to his incessant knocking. Father Jim rushed into the kitchen and demanded to see the sick parishioner.

"But there's nobody sick here, Father," protested the bewildered man of the house.

"Kneel down," cried the priest. "It doesn't matter a damn whether you're sick or not. I'm not coming out here again – even if I have to anoint every man, woman and child in the parish."

There were always stories doing the rounds. Like the time Father Jim, in the course of his pastoral duties, called on the old granny who lived alone in her smoke-filled hillside cottage. She had been drinking tea from a tin mug. Without washing it, she offered some to the priest. Now, for all his impatience, Father Jim was at heart a kind and sensitive man, and not wishing to offend the old lady, took the mug in his left hand and sipped from the opposite side. After some time, the old lady politely observed, "I see your reverence is left-handed like myself".

Life in the country in those days was different. Attitudes have changed and there is not the same sense of conservatism that was widespread and accepted in Father Jim's time. For instance, it was common enough to see an Oriental, I suspect Indian, gentleman, on a bicycle with a large suitcase, visiting houses throughout the countryside. The opened suitcase revealed a wide selection of spools of thread, elastic, hooks, needles, ribbons and sundry items for the lady of the house. No one refused him entry because they would not want the neighbours to say that they could not afford the wares on offer. But the dark gentleman was never entertained for too long, for fear that a nosey neighbour might suggest that there was something naughty going on. Strict propriety was the order of the day. In hilly country, the poor trader had to push his bicycle for a considerable part of the way. In hot weather he would have enjoyed a cup of tea, the traditional Irish custom, but this could only be offered if the man of the house was at home or the old granny was in the corner by the fire.

These memories of my impressionable teenage years were evoked as I continued my ramble along the abandoned railway track where O'Donnell's Rock was ablaze with blossoms of the prolific whitethorn. Though brief in time, these youthful memories belonged to that special period of life – when all the world was young and all the trees were green.

My emotional revisiting of days at Larkfield would leave its imprint: I was happy to once again attempt rejuvenation. It was in 1940 that we moved house to Larkfield, where I lived out my final teenage years.

Those were in many respects my most treasured years. It was a time of growing towards adulthood, full of hope and blissfully unaware that life is not the adventure we thought or planned. But then there was excitement in the air. Devastated and exhausted by four years of bloody war, the world, bewildered by the decimation of its youth, drew breath in 1918. Alas, it was only a pause until 1939 when the conflict resumed and shattered the peaceful innocent years of a new generation.

My time in Larkfield was the early years of that conflict. The outbreak of the Second World War was an uncertain time, and little did we know of the forthcoming events that would shape our lives in the years ahead. For now, we took what came our way and responded to events as they arose. Prime Minister DeValera broadcast an appeal for young men to rally to the colours by joining the Defence Forces. As teenagers, we could join the newly-formed Local Security Force, and in a burst of patriotic enthusiasm, or sheer bravado, we hastened to become the first recruits. I can well recall the perplexed local Garda's expression when four of us presented ourselves at the station for recruitment half an hour after DeValera's appeal. The good man, who had not heard the broadcast, did not know what we were talking about. But he did what was done – took our names and promised to let us know.

Within months, the Larkfield road resounded to the sound of marching feet. There was, surprisingly perhaps, a great response to the recruiting campaign, and men of all ages offered their services at the local Garda station. In those early years fifty or more men would assemble at St. Clare's Hall in the evening time and spend hours drilling and marching along the Larkfield road. At first there were no uniforms, rifles or other equipment, but that did not seem to matter very much as there was a great spirit of camaraderie and fellowship surrounding this exciting new venture. We marched for a few miles, fell out for a smoke and resumed the march homewards, singing our favourite songs of the day.

Our rented house on a small hillside about a mile outside the town was set well back from the road, on about two acres of ground, and was approached by a steep lane. Although not a very fine house, it had that most precious of attributes – location. The backdrop to our new home, in a peaceful sylvan setting, was the cliff-like mountain plateau of O'Donnell's Rock. An impressive feature of the landscape, and never more so than when ablaze with its golden furze and blossoming hawthorn, it rose sharply from the rear of the house Across the way, the land-mass of Benbo Mountain towered imposingly in the immediate distance. I may not have known it then, but I was certainly captivated by these silent, timeless sentinels that had for so long cast the spell of their ponderous presence over the landscape.

All around me were nature's blessings: song birds, wild life, hawthorn blossoms, primroses, bluebells and golden furze. It was a quiet countryside interrupted only by the infrequent trains of the SL&NCR puffing their way to Enniskillen or Sligo along the track across the fields and meadows at the front of the house.

Each step of my leisurely stroll took me past half-forgotten landmarks until, eventually, I came to the little laneway leading to my old home. Lingering at the rusty gate in the moss-covered pathway, I was captivated by precious memories associated with the abandoned old house. It was as if my sheep dog, Major, might suddenly come bounding down the lane to greet me and excitedly escort me to the house, past what was left of last year's reek of turf and this year's flowering potatoes, which I had sprayed with bluestone (copper sulphate) that morning.

In the wartime years of scarcity, there was great neighbourliness and support throughout the community. Our landlord was a good and kindly neighbour who gratuitously turned a few extra ridges of potatoes when ploughing a field adjacent to the house. I learned to cut the seed, spread the manure, lift the sod and insert the seeds, mould the young stalks and spray with bluestone to combat the dreaded potato blight. Later, there was the reward of harvesting the fruits of our labour from mother earth, and of always being close to nature.

Self-sufficiency was to be aimed at in those years, and securing the winter's fuel with a good supply of turf was a priority. I made my acquaintance with the bog. Bog country was usually very inaccessible as there were few roads into the interior of the bog. Consequently, the popular little donkeys were very much in demand. With two creels, a donkey could pick his way over the softest ground and find his way to the nearest road or cart track. Oh yes! The donkey was no fool. He knew were to put his feet.

The bog we had acquired was about half a mile as the crow flies from our house. It was inaccessible other than by donkey. I may not have thought of turf as the greatest thing on earth, or the highpoint of my days at Larkfield, but, contrary to some misconceptions, a day in the bog could be a very pleasing experience. It was there I witnessed the actual cutting of the turf, and I recall the skill of Pat the turf-cutter. He cut non-stop, seldom looking upwards, expertly flinging the soft peat overhead, to be caught and wheeled to the spreading-ground. Pat could cut a year's supply of turf in six days. The work was constant and little time was wasted for fear that the weather might break. There was, of course, a tea-break, and I recall my pleasure at the sight of my mother's blue apron in the distance as she came through the heather with her basket of sandwiches, hot tea, and other goodies. There was something very special about those days spent on the bog: the pure fresh air, the soft breeze on one's face, the smell of heather, the distinctive bog land plants, the sound of larks ascending, and the drone of insects. My days were far removed from that oft-portrayed derisory picture of life on the bog.

Pat was an excellent worker and was much in demand for all kinds of farm work. He was unmarried and lived with his widowed father, a pensioner from the First World War. They lived in an isolated cottage surrounded by boggy fields that were often flooded. As my friend Matt remarked, "A snipe would need wellingtons to get into that place."

From our kitchen window I had a commanding view of the surrounding countryside. Every Friday, pension day, as sure as day follows night, at about 2 o'clock, I would see Pat and his widowed father coming over the railway bridge on the road from town. Arm in arm, and much the worse for drink, father and son supported each other as they stumbled their happy way homeward, taking both sides of the road.

Thoughts of my faithful dog, Major, returned. He had been given to me as pup by a man whom I did not know very well. People were like that in Manorhamilton – friendly, thinking little of obliging or doing a turn, even to a mere acquaintance. I arrived home one Sunday morning holding one end of a rope with a playful young collie dog on the other end. At first there was some surprise but no objections from my mother. For the next fifteen years, and several house moves Major remained part of the household. He was a willing and adaptable traveller, endearing himself to family and visitors alike. And so the years rolled onwards until the day came when his blindness and old age forced us to put him to sleep. Heartbroken, I stood by as the vet inserted the needle and Major, as if in a final farewell gesture, tried to raise his head, gave a last feeble wag of his tail, and passed away.

I have a dream: the evening shadows falling over Larkfield, the leaves rustling in the soft summer breeze, and an old sheep dog waiting patiently by a rusty old iron gate. Perhaps I dream too much.

Chapter 13

Time to Leave

Feeling grateful for having had the opportunity of recapturing memories of those teenage years, I retraced my steps from Larkfield. The whitewashed walls of the old school building drowsed in the afternoon sunshine reviving memories of days at school, long hot summers and boyhood friends. Thankfully, it had withstood the ravages of time. Now a private dwelling, it remains a pointer to the past. For nearly one hundred years its classrooms resounded with laughter, tears and joy – and the sound of noisy footsteps, now dispersed along life's uncertain path.

I lingered on the bridge below the town, conjuring thoughts of half-forgotten schoolyard fights, fishing days and lazy homeward treks past the cobbler's shop which was once the *ceilidhe* house for half the town. The familiarity of it all had stirred deep memories, and I basked in the pleasant legacy of a vanished world. Although I knew that my rendezvous with those signposts to the past would soon end, the recollections of those early years had left an indelible imprint, and I fell to musing on what had been visited on our young war-time generation. Although fortunately spared the horrors of warfare, side effects were inevitable, there were food scarcities and rationing was introduced. As there was no petrol and very limited public transport, the trusty bicycle became king of the road. I reflected on the peace and quiet of the countryside around Larkfield at that time. The only intrusions were the sounds of wildlife, perhaps the barking of a distant dog or the peaceful sound of the mid-day Angelus bell and, from time to time, the puff-puff of a railway train on its way to Sligo or Enniskillen.

But there were occasional stark reminders of the closeness of war. It was early morning at Larkfield when I was awakened by an unusually loud noise. In haste I jumped from my bed and watched through the window in breathless amazement as a large RAF bomber winged its way perilously close to the house. It was obvious that the plane was in serious difficulty, and I recall my apprehension that it might crash. I watched as the plane - its crew clearly visible - skimmed past my bedroom window in wobbly flight towards the distant Ballyboy Hills, before disappearing from view across the border to its base near Enniskillen.

There was other evidence of the proximity of war: planes crashed in the mountain landscape of nearby Glenade and Glencar; the army arrived in town and established a base that remained for the duration of the war; young men joined the army or took employment across the border, where wartime activity had boosted the economy; and, despite the war or maybe because of it, many, however ill prepared, followed the well-worn emigration trail to Britain and booming employment opportunities. Almost by stealth, it seemed, as if our world had vanished. For those who remained, particularly those without land or inheritance, the future was bleak. This gradual loss of youthful companions, and an uncertain future, was the catalyst that prompted young blood to have its course, and go.

I recall how on a cold, bleak day in February 1942, with my eighteenth birthday behind me, I presented myself at the local Garda Station for enlistment in Óglaigh na hÉireann and bade good-bye to the fountain of my dreams. Time has dimmed recollections of my precise thoughts as I sat on that army lorry speeding across the plains of Roscommon to the recruiting depot at Athlone. Suffice it to say that like most young men I knew the time had come to make a break from home. I now suspect that when my contemporaries came home on leave their accounts of army experiences influenced my then restless and impatient spirit. These glowing accounts invariably painted a fulsome picture: how wonderful it was to have a regular pay-day and money in the pocket, dancing and opportunities to meet lovely girls, and the excitement of army life. There was never a reference to the downside of life in the army, but soon enough I discovered that life was not a bed of roses. For then however, I had the wondrous optimism of adventurous youth, and a naïve belief that a Pandora's Box would yield days of wine and glory.

My youthful impressions of those first days in the recruiting depot were reminiscent of scenes from First World War films: soldiers, crowded canteens, bellowing Sergeant Majors, military commands, platoons marching across the square, military bands, pompous officers, and lines of soldiers. Still in civilian clothes, I was anxious to shed my rookie status as soon as possible. Deliverance came when I was fitted out with the full regulation kit and I could return to anonymity in my bull's wool uniform.

The flat midland scenery of the Shannon watershed was no substitute for my beloved Larkfield, and thoughts of Benbo Mountain and O'Donnell's Rock were never far from my mind during those early days. But the new camaraderie bred new friendships, as the restless urge of youth sought new pastures. I have, of course, some nostalgia for those distant, golden days of youth – "when all the trees were green and every lass a queen" *

Nearly two years later, my enthusiasm for army life had become diminished by thirty-mile route marches, sweaty, bloody feet, endless manoeuvres, and a sense of boredom spawned by an uncertain future. When the opportunity came my way, I was happy to end my military career by joining the Garda Síochána in 1943.

All good things come to an end, and my extended sentimental journey would now become part of my memories. I have mixed feelings. Some elation filters through the nostalgia: memories of loved ones and loyal comrades. The Ireland of my youth made no promises, neither did it quench hope or a love of life, and the determination to take whatever opportunities might come my way.

Reluctantly, I set off on the return journey to Dublin, and as the train sped between the little towns I settled into my seat wistfully dreaming of my panorama of memories. I saw daffodils in bloom, and the closing lines of Wordsworth's poem came to mind

---

* Charles Kingsley

For oft when on my couch I lie
In vacant or in pensive mood,
They flash upon the inward eye,
Which is the bliss of solitude;
And then my heart with pleasure fills,
And dances with the daffodils.[*]

As the train sped onwards, my thoughts were of my brief visit home. By the time I arrived at my destination the resolve to continue my reminiscences had become irresistible. My reverie about my carefree youth urged me to recall and describe an eventful life thereafter, in the period from December 1943 to June 1984. My experiences may have been common-place. However, I will now re-live the simple joys and reveal some hidden facts of service in the Garda Síochána.

---

[*] William Wordsworth, *The Daffodils* (1815)

Chapter 14

First Days in the Force

It seems that I was destined to follow in my father's footsteps. Along with a new generation of recruits, I passed through the gates of the Garda Training Depot on 3rd December 1943. For any young man it was an exciting and important milestone. I had just turned twenty, and the world was my oyster. Forty-one years were to pass before I finally surrendered that fine blue uniform. The experiences of those four decades in the Dublin Metropolitan Division are tempered with mixed emotions.

I doubt if I ever thought very seriously about becoming a policeman – at least not until I was confronted with having to earn a living. At that stage, the war was coming to an end and the opportunities for employment were limited. Joining the Garda Síochána seemed an attractive alternative to further army service, until demobilisation came with its uncertain future. Besides, the nice blue uniform of the Garda Síochána seemed light-years ahead of the army's green 'bull's wool'. When you are just twenty years old, such considerations seem important.

Reflecting on those earlier years, it seems to me that we were living in an era which straddled two centuries, such was the slow pace of change since the early 1900s. I was twenty-one years of age when I graduated from the Garda Depot, and although I did not realise it at the time, the Garda Síochána, founded in 1922, was just a year older than I was. However, life in the Garda Síochána had changed little since the days of the RIC and the DMP. Half of the 20th Century would pass before there was any appreciable change in the character of the Force. Living conditions were very unsatisfactory, since most of the stations were, in fact, converted buildings which had been in use since the formation of the DMP back in 1836.

My first posting was to Irishtown, where the police were housed in a converted Coast Guard Station in Ringsend. It was here that I experienced the trauma of a young recruit's initiation into barrack life and the cultural shock of life on the streets of Dublin. The noise and bustle, the clanging of trams, the horse-drawn milk drays, the ubiquitous pawn-shop, the fish-and-chip shops, and the late-night revelling were foreign to a young man more familiar with the green fields, mountains, lakes and quiet life of the West of Ireland. The emotional ties of country life and the youthful dreams of a career as a rural Garda were about to be rudely shattered. Urban living and the city streets was my new domain.

Those first faltering steps along Ringsend Road brought me face-to-face with some buxom ladies, arms folded over ample breasts, silently contemplating the approaching new recruit. I was ten stone weight, and not quite the familiar burly figure of a seasoned DMP man. I was only too well aware of my lack of experience, but there was no escape for me. As I drew alongside, the ladies exclaimed in a strong Dublin accent, "Ah! God help him, sure he's only a chissler." Assuming an official pose I nonchalantly ambled past, inwardly fretting at my diminished status and hoping that, as the day progressed, my dignity would receive more recognition. Such thoughts, no doubt, were the lot of many young recruits on their first days on the beat.

But further trials lay ahead. It was my luck to have as my immediate superior the legendary Sergeant Denis Brady. My first impressions of this stocky individual in silver-buttoned long topcoat and Metropolitan police helmet, were of a rather comical figure, whose short bandy legs might conceivably fail him as he mounted his 'high Nelly' bicycle. His antics sometimes bordered on the bizarre, and at times seemed to defy reason. Indeed, he could well have come straight from the pages of a Charles Dickens novel. Although not evil or malicious in character, his comments were often laced with a perverse sense of humour.

Like most young men, I was anxious to shed the embarrassment of the rookie cop and to integrate with the older hands as quickly as possible. But Brady would have none of it. Much to my annoyance he persisted in always referring to me to me as "the recruit." "Did anyone see the recruit?" were the words I heard on every occasion. I had hoped that my torment would end with the arrival of a new recruit some six months later. Surely the new man would henceforth fill the role for Sergeant Brady? But nothing doing. He had decided that I should now be referred to as the "senior recruit" and the new man as the "junior recruit". Rapid promotion, indeed!

There are other unforgettable characters from those early years that remain fresh in my memory. There was Charlie, the Special Branch man, who hung his loaded Webley revolver by the trigger guard on a nail in his food locker. Particles of decayed food were embedded in the bullet chamber, and I doubt if it had been unloaded for the entire duration of the Second World War. I was always nervous when Charlie came to dine.

Then there was Peter with whom I shared a bedroom. As well as a great lover of porter - as evidenced by an accumulation of empty bottles under his bed – Peter had an obsession with the war. Armed with a goodly supply of English newspapers and wearing his faded Long Johns, he climbed into bed on Sunday afternoons. From a horizontal position, he would excitedly forecast the outcome of the most recent military campaign during my attempts to get some sleep following a tour of night duty. The living and working conditions were such that Sergeant Brady became the least of my concerns, and I resolved to distance myself as soon as possible from Irishtown, with its fly-infested mess-room and the official issue of 1912 blankets.

And so began my love affair with Dalkey, that quaint, old-world Viking village on the fringe of Dublin's teeming megalopolis. Other than being the destination of the No. 8 tram, Dalkey was a place about which I knew absolutely nothing at that time. Having grown up in the West of Ireland, I would have preferred a posting to some rural station, in line with my pre-conceived ideas of life in the Garda Síochána. But I might as well have sought holy water in an Orange Lodge, as a transfer to a rural station was out of the question at that particular time. By such slender threads hangs life's destiny, and who knows how life might have unfolded for me in the outer regions of Donegal or West Cork?

I was destined to spend almost my entire service between the mountains and the sea in the elegant Borough of Dún Laoghaire-Rathdown. Here, as in the Force, the winds of change were but slowly blowing, and such was the pace of change that in 1945 I was occasionally being addressed as *Constable*, and sometimes given a *Kingstown* address.[*]

My early enchantment with the area stemmed from the little harbours, the quaint houses, the splendid scenery, the sense of antiquity, and the faded imprints of its Viking past. The neat gardens, the elegant period houses with tiny lodges and resident gardeners, coloured my village beat. Many of these have long since vanished – as has the lifestyle they supported.

Now, the village of Dalkey at the time of my arrival in the final months of the Second World War was a quiet backwater, very different from the affluent dormitory town it has now become. I well recall my pleasure at first sighting the Garda Station on the quiet Sorrento Road in April 1945. It had been a typical two-storey private dwelling before being utilised as a police station by the DMP and had remained unspoiled and quite unlike a police station with its aesthetic iron railings and a small front garden of purple herbal shrubs. The little office, with ancient grandfather clock, high wooden desk and a quaint swinging half-door were relics of another age.

A pleasant sergeant greeted me warmly with a firm handshake and a friendly welcome. Instinctively, I felt at home, and in the years that followed I fell in love with the place. It was all very much to my liking, and I quickly adapted to my new surroundings, making many friends in the local community, and enjoying the birdsong at dawn that chorused on Sorrento Road on summer mornings. Indeed, this was a long way from the downbeat environment of my first year at Irishtown.

Those early years gave me endless satisfaction, as a young man, viewing the delights of Dalkey and Killiney. The nature of our work

---

[*] "Kingstown" was, of course, the colonial name for Dún Laoghaire and "Constable" the form of address under English rule.

patrolling the district by day and by night inculcated a sense of involvement in the area. Acquiring a good local knowledge came easily and I was soon conscious of such place names as Vico, Sorrento, Monte Alverno, Mount Etna, and San Elmo. I could have been in the Bay of Naples! It was a welcome fringe benefit to my new position in life – a sort of busman's holiday. I was being paid to walk through some of the most wonderful scenery in Ireland. Sometimes I thought that I might be the envy of tourists and day-trippers, as I strolled along the beautiful Vico Road, the neighbouring hills of Killiney and Dalkey, or savoured the delights of Sandycove. In addition, a man of high integrity, Michael Lawlor, who had joined the DMP in 1912, took much pride and pleasure in passing on to me his knowledge of local history. Many years later, I came to greatly appreciate the little gems of local history he so readily imparted – and which are not always to be found in the pages of history books.

In those days a stately old house, in its final years of decay, stood at the top of Albert Road on the site of the present traffic roundabout below Avondale Road. Known originally as *Sion House* it was the residence of two sisters of Charles Stewart Parnell, the 'uncrowned King of Ireland', whose home was at Avondale in Co. Wicklow. On Victoria Road in Dalkey I found the former residence of Michael Davitt, founder of the Land League. Also, I learned of Sandycove's association with the poet Padraig Colum as well as with the executed 1916 leader, Roger Casement, and the writers A. G. Strong and Monk Gibbon.

At Killiney I discovered the reputed seat of the ancient druids. Here an enterprising local publican had coined the colourful name, *The Druid's Chair*, for his licensed premises nearby. An effervescent colleague, the late Pat Cahillane, always referred to this publican as The Chief Druid.

Killiney held for me a special fascination – a sort of magical appeal – especially when patrolling it in the quietness of a fine moonlit-night. As there was little or no traffic in those days, night duty offered something of a relief. We were less involved in the day-to-day affairs of the station and when the world had gone to bed we had freedom to relax on our patrol. On reaching the top of Killiney Hill Road at around 3:30 am, and gazing down on the twinkling city slumbering below, I was happy in the stillness of the night to relax with a lighted pipe and contemplate my surroundings. The Obelisk erected on the summit of Killiney Hill by landlord John Mapas in 1742 to give much-needed employment to the poor is a reminder of famine times. From here can be seen the old Union Workhouse at Shanganagh, now part of Loughlinstown Hospital. The workhouses were all of similar design, and the sight of the Shanganagh building always stirred memories of my youthful days at Manorhamilton.

Dalkey Hill and its environs had by this time cast a spell over me. There was an awakening to the charm of my new environment and its urban-village life. Here, as we peacefully went our daily way, were the narrow hilly streets of a quaint old place. The small cottages with half-doors and small windows were typical of what I had seen in the West of Ireland. At first I was unsure of their origin – they seemed so out-of-place in this urban setting. Later I learned something of their history as homes of the migrant quarry workers who hewed the granite from Dalkey Quarry to build Dúnlaoghaire Pier. Those cliffs of the granite quarry on Dalkey Hill cast shadows from other days. There still remained the tiny cabin-like houses built by migrant workers near the quarry where they sought refuge from hunger in the rural Ireland of the 1840s. By the flagstones in Ardbrugh Road were the lingering traces of the cable-car track used in the construction of Dún Laoghaire's magnificent harbour, constructed from 1817 to 1842.

Locky's off-licence was an oddly-shaped single-storey building on Ardbrugh Road, surrounded by even odder little houses, and far removed from the grandiose drinking emporia of today. It was a quiet, sunny afternoon when I first crossed the threshold to innocently purchase a packet of cigarettes. My uniformed presence surprised the proprietor and the sole customer, a startled bread deliveryman. The deliveryman was enjoying his pint of Guinness while in deep conversation with the proprietor. Their conversation ceased and a deadly silence prevailed as, feeling a bit like Gary Cooper in *High Noon,* I paced the long bare wooden floor leading to the counter at the far end of the shop. I noticed that Locky had deftly concealed the visitor's pint behind his newspaper. The consumption of drink on the premises was, of course, a breach of the licensing laws. I am glad to recall that I chose to ignore both the pint and the evident discomfiture of the two men. Confining myself to an exchange of pleasantries on the fine weather we were having, I departed with my packet of cigarettes. Sadly, Locky ceased to trade many years ago.

Once upon a time, Ardbrugh was a little village in its own right and, as Locky's was originally a 19th century inn catering for the quarry-workers, it may well have been known as Ardbrugh Inn. At the time of my arrival in Dalkey it was licensed only as an 'off-licence' and was popular with some of the locals on Good Fridays and other 'closed dates'. It was popular also, of course, during the 'holy hour' when the pubs were obliged to close between 2:30 pm and 3:30 pm. Whatever about its drinking facilities, the building proved attractive to Harry Kernoff RHA, whose fine painting in 1936 of the old building has recently been valued at €20,000.

Nearby Torca Road brings back memories of the unveiling of a commemorative plaque to the memory of George Bernard Shaw, at Torca Cottage, where he resided for some years. The Dalkey Development Association had it erected there in 1947. It bears Shaw's words, "The men of Ireland are mortal, but her hills are eternal." Having enjoyed the pleasures of the twin hills of Killiney and Dalkey for over half a century, I can well appreciate the appropriateness of Shaw's quotation. Fortunately, unlike Locky's off-licence, the plaque survives the ravages of time.

Regular patrols on clearly defined beats were performed under strict supervision over the twenty-four-hour period. The regularity and consistency of these patrols was, I am sure, comforting to the residents and helped to foster good relations with the community. Our daily duties were at the 'coalface' of village life. We shared the streets with postmen, tram drivers and conductors, council workers, hospital staff, ambulance-men, firemen, railway staff, and many others. From this sense of fellowship came spontaneous cooperation. There are abiding memories of warm friendships and camaraderie, not to mention the numerous characters and incidents, which are now all part of folk memory.

Ma Reilly's unusual little shop was located in the centre of Castle Street, the main street of the village. It was unusual for the fact that customers were never allowed to enter the shop, as all business was conducted by Ma through a partially opened door onto the street. Customers, it seemed, were happy enough to stand in all kinds of weather and to receive their daily paper from Ma who stood almost hidden inside and kept one half of the door slightly ajar. Money was handed in and the paper handed out through the opening. Describing it as a Newsagents would be an overstatement. Ma was a widow of advanced years. She lived alone over the shop – though this is hard to say for certain, as nobody ever got in there. She had carried on business there for many years and her origins were something of a mystery. Rumour had it that her husband was a member of the RIC and that she came from Co. Tyrone. Always dressed in long black clothes, she could have stepped out of a Victorian drama. A novel feature was a sort of 'bird's nest' bundle enclosed in a net which hung half way down her back. Some said that it contained all her money.

For those of us Guards whom she might permit to gaze further into her domain, a scene of mounds of newspapers piled to ceiling height was unveiled. This was topped by all sorts of sweet-cans, baskets, magazines and an assortment of long outdated household items. But it was the foul air, permeated with the perfume of cat's urine, wafting towards the partially opened door from inside that dulled any curiosity that might have arisen on being afforded the rare opportunity of getting inside. Of course, the place was a fire trap, but in those times no action was ever contemplated by the authorities.

Chapter 15

The Rare Old Times

As the Second World War was drawing to a close, a few years would pass before the seemingly permanent signs of the country's struggle to survive passed into history. When I was at the Garda Training Depot, our early-morning run was overshadowed by the giant ricks of damp and mouldy turf which lined our route through the Phoenix Park. They were a pitiful source of fuel for the citizens of Dublin for over five years. Likewise, the stinking air-raid shelters, then a feature of many streets, remained long after the need had ceased to exist.

However, the partial blackout restrictions, then in force, were immediately lifted at the end of the war. A total blackout had been imposed at the outbreak of war in 1939. Almost immediately, the German government made it clear that Germany would not be responsible if any of its bombs fell on Irish territory. This, it was claimed, was on account of German aircraft being unable to distinguish a blacked-out Ireland from a blacked-out Britain.

The British government had a different view. The absence of a blackout in Ireland created a beacon by which the German bombers could pinpoint their bombing raids on Britain. And so the argument flowed in the early days of the war. Eventually, a compromise was reached – there would be a partial blackout. Cowls were placed on all public lampposts, and restrictions imposed on public lighting generally. It was a classical Irish solution to an Irish problem.

Every time I now pass along Northumberland Road, I am reminded of my early days at Irishtown. It was here, outside No. 58, that I paced for many hours in front of what was then the German Legation in Ireland. Dr. Hempel, the German Ambassador, would arrive most days accompanied by his aides. Ever courteous and polite, he never failed to acknowledge our salute with a wave of his hand. Likewise, the staff at the Legation always exchanged formal greetings with those of us on duty. It was a very important assignment, a most sensitive one requiring round-the-clock protection, and a post never to be vacated unless one was properly relieved.

I had been on duty one day at the Legation for about five hours, until relieved at 7.00 pm. It so happened that on this occasion my relief was none other than "Lobsters" Doran the latest recruit to arrive at Irishtown. By coincidence, Lobsters, a Dubliner, had been a schoolmate of mine in St. Mary's College, Dundalk in the late 30s. Schoolboys are renowned for their deftness in giving nicknames. In this case, it was soon discovered when Doran arrived at St. Mary's that his family were in the fish business. From then onwards he was known as Lobsters.

As I sat down to tea in Irishtown that evening, I became aware of great commotion in the station office, where the Sergeant was in a panic. The word was that the German Legation had been attacked. Apparently, shortly after I had finished my stint there, an excited individual jumped off the No.8 tram, unfolded a newspaper as he walked past the unsuspecting Lobsters and, determined to strike a blow for freedom against Hitler, hurled a brick through a window of the Legation building. Fortunately for those on duty, the culprit was immediately arrested and taken to Irishtown station. I cannot recall the outcome of this incident, but it is safe to say that a major international crisis did not arise. Adolph Hitler had other things on his mind in 1944.

From time to time, we were directed to make a public display of law enforcement. This usually took the form of a brief, sudden purge of those transgressing the traffic laws. Now, in 1944 there was very little traffic other than the thousands of cyclists who daily thronged the city streets. The apparent sudden zeal for law and order stemmed more from pressure by the local superintendent, anxious to ensure a good return of summonses from his district, than from any great enthusiasm on our part. The flotillas of unlit bicycles were always a fertile and easy source for summonses.

Merrion Road was usually designated a suitable place for such hold-ups. I recall a late Sunday evening in September when I had my first experience with unlit bicycles. It had been a wonderful summer's day and thousands of cyclists were returning from a day out at the seaside in Dún Laoghaire and Blackrock. The road was thronged with cyclists, nearly all without lights, and Sergeant Brady was directing operations. From the middle of the road with outstretched arms, as if herding cattle, he faced the oncoming waves of happy citizens. Now, Sergeant Brady was an unusual man who seemed to delight in the use of unusual language. On this occasion, he challenged the offending cyclists: "Why are you riding this machine on the President's highway without a light?" I was getting to know Sergeant Brady.

Needless to say, our more seasoned members took these operations as a matter of course by largely ignoring Sergeant Brady and leaving him to enjoy his antics. If names were taken few summonses were issued. It was wartime, batteries were almost impossible to obtain, and we used our commonsense.

Somewhat more amusing are my memories of the official line on wartime policing. The war was, of course, an entirely new ball game without precedent and with few guidelines for those charged with issuing orders or giving directions. Following the bombing of the North Strand in 1940, it was thought fit to issue an instruction for the guidance of men on beat duty. This was to the effect that, "In the event of an air-raid taking place, while on beat duty, members may take temporary shelter, but should resume patrolling immediately the air raid has ceased." I heard a story from a senior member of the Force that, in the immediate aftermath of bombs being dropped on Sandycove, a very high-ranking officer, when he arrived on the scene, saw fit to reprimand him for not having removed his bicycle clips.

Another story going the rounds in those days centred on arrangements for the Local Security Force (LSF), which had been formed to assist the Garda Síochána in the first year of the war. Members of the LSF regularly patrolled the district in pairs at night time. On one occasion, a member of this night patrol reported that German U Boats had been observed off Dún Laoghaire. The alarm raised by this report required an immediate call-out, and the arming of the Local Security Force. Ammunition for such an emergency was normally kept under lock and key. When the local unit had assembled it was discovered that the key to the ammunition press was with the off-duty Staff Sergeant at his home in Sandycove. A cyclist was urgently dispatched to procure the key, so that military resistance to the threat of German U Boats could be initiated. We were in another world.

Of course, we had our own quota of characters in those days. There was 'Ikey' the tram conductor noted for his wit, short temper, and quick response. When some local wags, standing near a tram stop, cried out: "Did you pass a lorry load of monkeys on your way," there came the quick retort, "Why? Did you fall off"?

Many of the tram conductors were noted for their good humour and wit. They would helpfully call out the location of some important tram-stops. The film "Waterloo Bridge" was showing in the Astoria and as the tram approached the cinema in Glasthule conductor 'Twilight' Kavanagh usually cried out: "Anyone for Waterloo Bridge."

Then we had Frank, the Sergeant, who seemed transfixed whenever a member of the fair sex entered the station. I was hastily brushed aside one day as Frank rushed to attend to the glamorous and sophisticated young lady who came to the office. Deirdre, for that was her name, was seeking information relating to a recent traffic accident. When requested by Frank if she could give the investigating Garda's number, her languid and rather sultry response came slowly, "Oh! I don't know his number, but I can tell you that he has the most wonderful pair of brown eyes." A highly excited Frank exploded with the rather unenthusiastic response "I mean to say, in this office we go more by their District Number than by the colour of their eyes." I am not sure how the sultry Deidre responded, or how far the brown eyed Garda pursued his inquiries.

On another occasion a somewhat haughty lady phoned to say that a valuable duck had strayed into her garden.

Frank inquired, "Can you say, madam, if the bird is a duck or a drake?"

Then there came the shrill and annoyed response, "How would I know if it is a duck or a drake?"

But, Frank was not to be fazed, "I mean to say, can you say if it is in an exhausted condition?"

The lady's response is better left to the imagination.

Each generation will have its very own version of "the rare old times," and as the years steal away there comes the tempting call of nostalgia, sometimes cynically referred to as 'history with the bad parts taken out.' At such times, I welcome the freedom to choose what I may, or may not, recall. While it is pleasant to bask in the warmth of selected memories I am only too well aware that the reality may have been somewhat different. Time always brings change, and as we grow older we tend to be distrustful of 'change.' The old times seemed better, the summer days longer, the weather finer, the trees greener, the food tasted better, life was more leisurely and there was more courtesy. However, perhaps at the time this was not really so.

The annual Spring Show in May and the Horse Show in August, at the Royal Dublin Society (RDS) in Ballsbridge, was a matter of some pride for those on duty there. We paraded in our special navy blue dress uniform of those days. This comprised a traditional police helmet, high-neck tunic – with a single row of silver buttons, a silver buttoned rear pleat, and a black leather belt with a silver buckle. We all wore snow-white gloves for the occasion, which entailed a man on traffic duty at every junction at the approaches to the RDS. It was a scene worthy of an artist's canvas – the tall white-gloved policemen standing erect in the centre of the roadway, amidst a profusion of flowering cherry trees, as an impatient flow of horses, cars, lorries, vans, and bicycles speed to their destination. The dress uniform and the style of policing of those days have now both vanished. While the Royal Dublin Society and the Ballsbridge area are no longer redolent of those days, the cherry blossoms thankfully still bloom.

Like many of the buildings and the style of life, most of the street characters of those years have vanished from the scene. We encountered them every day and every night. Dan Nevin was one of these and he seemed to have been around forever. He was a harmless poor man, who never caused trouble to anyone. Like most destitute men, he slept rough outdoors in the summertime, usually along the seafront at Dún Laoghaire, and during the wintertime in the Morning Star and the

Iveagh Hostels. Dan was always grateful for the gift of our cast-off uniform trousers, as well as the occasional odd job or few shillings we could pass his way. He was my first experience of such unfortunate people without home or shelter and, frustratingly, there seemed so little we could do about it.

"Slippers" was a real eccentric. Unlike Dan Nevin, he seemed to have independent means. He lived alone in a nice detached bungalow in the vicinity of Dalkey Hill. From here he would cycle to Dublin and beyond on his racing sports bicycle. Head down, he would pedal furiously, as he weaved his way through the streets in all kinds of weather. Now, his eccentricity was not the healthy practice of cycling, but his style of dress and his seeming indifference to all around him. His dress invariably consisted of a knotted handkerchief as headdress, a pair of off-white long johns, knitted ankle-socks and a flimsy blue-striped nightshirt. Regardless of the weather, he always wore a pair of badly-worn black slippers and a glazed cape – sometimes yellow, sometimes black. He had designed a form of windscreen from the lid of a plywood tea chest. This was mounted on the handlebars by means of metal tubes and a series of bolts and nuts. A selection of colourful ribbons, plastic toy propellers and two or three bells completed his list of accessories – optional extras if you like. Slippers would fly past at break-neck speed, peddling like a bat out of hell and bound for God-knows-where. He seldom stopped or dismounted from his bicycle, and we knew very little of his business. His sudden arrival on the streets of Dalkey was of little surprise to local people, but was always a source of mild amusement to those seeing him for the first time.

Then there was Jessie, whose husband was killed in the Great War. The poor soul never quite got over the death of her husband. For many years afterwards she insisted on appearing on the street dressed in her very own version of military uniform. This usually consisted of a three-quarter-length bright-blue tunic-type coat, with two rows of brass buttons. A self-styled military cap topped her ensemble, which conjured visions of Crimean War veterans, or Chelsea Pensioners.

Jessie was the source of some concern to me during my first weeks on the beat in her area. She insisted on standing in the middle of the street, regardless of the traffic. Suddenly she would march about twenty paces up the centre of the roadway and perform a drill routine. This comprised a series of left and right turns, coming smartly to attention, then a sharp about-turn and a march off down the centre of the roadway to her original position. During these military manoeuvres she recited various commands to herself while oblivious to all and sundry.

At first I was unsure of what exactly I should do with this *prima donna* who insisted on parading in front of me, as I did not have a clue as to her background. I was apprehensive that she might come to some harm in the course of her routine or become a nuisance to others. Although the traffic was not of to-day's density, I was constantly in dread that Jessie might throw herself onto the tram-tracks in front of an oncoming tram. I need not have worried: the local populace was well used to Jessie's antics and little concern was expressed by anybody. Likewise, although the trams on their fixed rails allowed no room for manoeuvre, the drivers had come to know of Jessie and would always slow down whenever she was in the vicinity. I never took any action, never received a complaint, and Jessie lived to a ripe old age.

There was also Chauser who was a neighbour of Jessie's in those days. He was an enormously fat man, and could barely walk on account of his great weight, said to be in excess of twenty stone. He, too, like Jessie's husband, had been a soldier in the First World War. He was in receipt of a disability pension for shellshock. As was the practice, every so often he was medically assessed to confirm that his condition justified the continued payment of his pension. On one such occasion, the medical board were in some doubt as to the *bona fides* of his claim and sought further reports on his condition, thereby implying that he might indeed be in full command of all his faculties. On getting wind of what was brewing, Chauser emerged from his small dwelling off the main street one afternoon in his 'birthday suit'. He waddled down the street; all twenty stone, wearing only his slippers, and took his position in the queue at the first tram stop he reached. The impact of his dramatic appearance among local shoppers is not difficult to imagine. Chauser was whisked away by ambulance, and a full report on the matter later found its way to the War Pensions Board. Chauser continued to receive his pension until he died many years later.

In the course of time we made personal friends and developed close relationships. I recall my friend John who was the personification of the DIY (Do It Yourself) cult. When John retired from the ESB, his first priority was his woodshed – a lean-to construction at the end of his garden. He installed electricity, a woodturning lathe and – I kid you not – a home-brewing still which he had contrived from old beer kegs and copper pipes.

To rendezvous with John one approached this multi-purpose woodshed via the rear lane. To gain entry you had to be *au fait* with his security system. This consisted of two screws in the top of the door-frame wired to a bell within. By short circuiting the screws with a coin you signalled John of the arrival of an intimate friend. When November came, I usually supplied John with sacks of crab apples acquired on my visits to the country. These he enthusiastically converted into an excellent beverage – call it wine if you wish. But he also distilled whiskey and brewed beer. However well intentioned, a brief visit to John's woodshed often turned into a very sociable, if protracted, social occasion.

Sadly, my friend John passed away some years ago. So nowadays when I drive past the laneway leading to his quaint old woodshed I have fanciful thoughts of his little 'Speak-easy' – and almost savouring the sweet smelling aroma of wood shavings, apples, sawdust and – "what ever you're having yourself."

Such characters and incidents were part of our daily experience while policing the streets of Dublin. Undoubtedly, many of my colleagues have recollections of similar characters to embellish tales of those rare old times.

Chapter 16

What's in a Name?

During those first years I soon became aware of the culture which had evolved in the Force ever since the days of the DMP. You were seldom called by your name but addressed by your District Number. Indeed, you almost ceased to exist as a person with a name. 'Tell 121 that he's wanted in the office' or, 'Call 79 to the phone', are examples of the everyday language that was inherited from the early days of the DMP. Fortunately, such enumeration was absent throughout the rest of the Garda Síochána in provincial Ireland.* While it may have been simpler to use numbers instead of names, there were times you felt that maybe you no longer had a name. Perhaps Sergeant Frank was not too far off the mark when he informed the glamorous young lady who asked to see the Guard with the brown eyes: "We go more by District Numbers than we do by the colour of their eyes."

However, as in all institutions, we had our quota of individuals who attracted the appendage of a nickname. At Dalkey, some were known in local public jargon as 'The Cat', 'The Captain', and so on, and we had our own 'honours list.' The Captain had served in the army prior to joining the Garda, and in true military tradition was still referred to as Captain – some thirty years later. The Cat had been so nicknamed by local wags who claimed that he always wore rubber-soled shoes while silently patrolling the streets – like a cat. Mac's Smile was a well-known brand of razor-blade at the time. Its logo depicted a grumpy, unshaven man which, when inverted, turned out to be the face of a smiling well-shaven gentleman. We had a rather grumpy old sergeant by the name of Mac, who seldom smiled, but constantly fussed over the most trivial

---

* Numbers were later introduced for all uniformed personell.

details. He was simply known as 'Mac's Smile'

'The Saw' had an immutable style when expounding on any recent experience. He would drone on and on, in a monotonous tone, like the sound from a carpenter's saw – hence the nickname.   Prior to the monthly court session, The Saw would delight in long and explicit in-depth discussion on the merits of his upcoming case. After court proceedings, he was more than eager to engage on any point of law which might have arisen – and which you might be foolish enough to mention. Among his colleagues, the view was sometimes humorously expressed that he would have made an excellent High Court judge.

Following an operation for the removal of his appendix, The Saw indulged in detailed retelling of the event. A casual and innocent onlooker could be forgiven for believing that The Saw had recently qualified in medicine – specifically in surgery.   Indeed, it was sometimes alleged that The Saw would say Mass if called upon to do so. He professed to have the ear of the local parish priest, and to be on very intimate terms with him. Indeed, he always referred to him as Paul - not Father Paul, mind you.

For the Garda seeking to curry favour, or to pick up what crumbs might fall from the table, Dalkey had few crumbs to offer. It was a small station, and there was very limited scope for granting privileges. But Ankles was a man prone to flattering conversation with the higher ranks – and he was usually given 'soft' assignments. Being a new man in Dalkey, I was often curious about the origins of those nicknames. When I asked the origin of his unusual nickname, a colleague given to colourful language explained: "Ah! You see, Ankles is so far up the Sergeant's arse, all you ever see of him are his ankles."

Then there was Sergeant Tom Collins, who was directed, while on night duty, to take charge of a rather unusual case at the old Monkstown Hospital. The Sergeant at Blackrock received a midnight call for help on behalf of a rather distraught student, to the effect that his testicles had been locked with a steel padlock. The disbelieving Sergeant, sensing a hoax, put down the phone immediately. Minutes later the call was repeated and the Sergeant, by nature a cautious man, decided to take the matter seriously and directed Collins to investigate.

So Sergeant Tom, a seasoned man of much commonsense, found himself at Monkstown Hospital, where the student had been taken – complete with locked padlock. It seems that fellow-students had, by way of a prank, 'secured' their colleague's testicles with a padlock, but unfortunately had lost the key. Sergeant Collins procured a strong hacksaw and tediously cut through the padlock, under the supervision of a youthful intern – and two young nurses. The operation was declared an unqualified success, and Sergeant Collins from that night onwards was known as Surgeon Collins.

Joe was made an official driver in the early 1950s, shortly after the introduction of District patrol cars. This was regarded as one of the cushy jobs, usually much sought after in those days, as it took you off your feet, and afforded protection in inclement weather. So there was usually some competition and 'string-pulling' involved. When a vacancy arose, much to the surprise of everyone, Joe got the job. Not, I hasten to add, because of his driving skills. Joe certainly was no sycophant, but he did have some influence.

I would regularly accompany Joe, as stand-by driver, on the routine journey to Dublin Castle to deliver mail and get a refill of petrol at the official pumps. Yes, it was an extraordinarily inefficient use of resources. But my problem was not so much with the system, as with Joe's driving. To drive in second gear from Dún Laoghaire to Dublin Castle, a distance of seven miles, without once changing gear, was a feat which only Joe could perform. However, there were other features of his driving skills that led to even greater embarrassment – mostly poor parking skills, resulting in minor damage to the bodywork of the patrol car.

Making official reports on such incidents became so embarrassing that Joe resorted to the rather unorthodox precaution of concealing a heavy lump-hammer under the driver's seat. With this hammer he was known to have performed many secretive minor running repairs – not always up to professional standards.

A story goes that, having driven past a carelessly parked bread van, in a burst of enthusiasm Joe decided to prosecute. However, in the course of completing a U-turn to return to the stationary bread van he misjudged his distance, struck a low wall and jammed his rear bumper against a metal post. He was now wedged in such a position that he could neither drive forward nor backward, without the certainty of causing further damage to the patrol car. There was nothing for it but the hammer. As Joe was endeavouring to free the trapped patrol car, and much to the embarrassment of James, his observer, the offending van driver pulled alongside, and hailing Joe in a friendly voice cried out, "Can I be of any help, gentlemen?"

On another occasion he parked the patrol car on the busy main street at Blackrock, very close - too close - to an ESB pole. After some time, he attempted to drive off again. However, in the meantime, unnoticed by Joe, a lorry had pulled in and parked rather close, behind the patrol car. Pulling and tugging the steering wheel Joe had great difficulty extracting himself from an embarrassing predicament on the main street. In the course of much swearing and frustration he eventually succeeded exclaiming in a loud voice, "Will you look where they put the bloody ESB poles." Until his retirement he was known as The Hammer.

As this is all on the lighter side of life in those days at Dalkey, I feel that I might conclude with reference to what may be described as something of a diplomatic incident. It concerns one of the older members attached to Dalkey at the time of my arrival there.

Tom was one of the first generation of Guards. He had joined the DMP and later was amalgamated into the Garda Síochána. He was a quiet man – seldom seen and little heard. At the time of my arrival, he had secured for himself a cosy niche by way of special duty at the Carlisle Pier in Dún Laoghaire. He performed no other duties, never paraded with the rest of us, and by and large had little to do, other than supervise the arrival and departure of passengers. Because of his confined duties, Tom had acquired a degree of anonymity. He had absolutely no experience of the normal administrative procedures in the day-to-day running of the Force, and indeed had no inclination whatever in that direction. In fact, he had perfected an extremely guarded approach to all forms of paper work, and would go to great lengths to avoid any possibility of such involvement unless absolutely obliged to do so. This phobia – for that was what it was – went as far as having family members collect his weekly pay or apply for leave on his behalf. He obviously had a great reluctance to put pen to paper. Indeed, as far as the rest of us were concerned, he might have been 'The Invisible Man.'

In those days, the State mailbags arrived, under armed escort, at Dún Laoghaire Pier. For some unexplained reason, Tom found himself at the heart of a rare and serious investigation into the loss of what was known as The Diplomatic Bag. This bag had been labelled for the British Embassy, but had somehow been delivered elsewhere by mistake. There followed a high-powered investigation to discover the cause and, of course, to fix responsibility. The file travelled its circuitous route for over eighteen months, as there was the usual sidestepping, buck-passing, and, of course, the need to find a scapegoat. Eventually, somebody thought of Tom. He was duly confronted and asked to give an account of his duties at the pier. Reluctantly, he submitted a very brief account of his daily routine and hoped that this would be the end of the matter.

However, the file kept coming back to Tom, thus drawing him deeper and deeper into the bureaucratic quagmire. Some of his responses, to a variety of petty and apparently irrelevant issues, were deemed unsatisfactory. Becoming increasingly frustrated and fearful of the whole distasteful business and in the hope of ending his involvement, Tom finally admitted to a minor error. Besides, he had other things on his mind — such as the renewal of his uniform. Being far from *au fait* with office procedures, and hoping to kill two birds with the one stone, Tom's historic few lines read, "I regret having inadvertently misunderstood the question and, now that I have the pen in my hand, I wish to apply for a pair of trousers." Apparently he had more important matters than Her Majesty's correspondence on his mind.

Chapter 17

Feet on the Street

No doubt, there was a lot of boredom – as well as hardship involved in 'pounding the beat.' But patrolling the streets was seen as the primary feature of police life in those days, and it was the lot of the great majority of the Force for most of their careers. The reassuring presence of police on the streets was considered fundamental to the maintenance of law and order. Certainly, a more visible presence of Gardaí nowadays would be high in most people's priorities. Increasingly, I hear serious and conscientious citizens, especially the elderly, deplore the lack of a visible police presence in our cities and towns.

For the duration of my service, the emphasis was certainly on having men on the streets. Monthly leave was often cancelled if there were not sufficient men available to man the beats – especially at night-time. Some officers would even prohibit the granting of leave on Saturday nights in order to ensure shift strengths for beat duty. This was, of course, a cause of some discontent, and I recall feeling obliged to make appropriate representations to our local Superintendent on at least one occasion. Saturday night was regarded as important for week-end activities, as well as being at home with our families, if at all possible.

Nowadays, the emphasis seems to be on specialisation, whether it be drugs, traffic, protection duty, or any of the many other assignments considered necessary in an increasingly complex society. The absence of men on the beat has contributed to a sense of isolation in the Garda Síochána, as it has diminished the opportunities for personal contact with citizens. It has, sadly, brought about a remoteness from ordinary people that is foreign to the traditions of the Force, and has fostered a sort of 'them and us' mentality. In spite of schemes to develop community policing, such as Neighbourhood Watch, and Community Alert, there is no longer the same sense of security as when patrolling

Gardaí were a regular feature of police life. No doubt, the pace of life, the increased demands on Gardaí, and the need to ensure fair and acceptable standards of industrial relations for the Force, place a greater strain on manpower. Nevertheless, the need for a return to a visible police presence on the streets, and an increased personal contact with the public, is self-evident. Unless there is a return to clearly visible policing, attitudes towards law and order will continue to deteriorate. The task of the Garda Síochána will become even more difficult, and society, as a whole will be the loser.

There has evolved over the years, a diminution in the status of on the beat policing. The routine nature of the work is perceived as unchallenging, and, indeed, there were always those who aspired to other duties and were regarded as soft-job men. Not always the most popular with the majority of their colleagues, they managed to avoid regular duty, and were often in receipt of extra money by way of allowances. The need for increased mobility, the availability of new technology, and the changed environment in which we live, have been offered as reasons for the absence of guards on such duty. But police on the beat have traditionally been lauded as the heart of policing all over the world. Status and self-esteem, which is largely shaped by official attitudes and policy, is fundamental to the public perception and self-image of the Force as a whole.

My recollections of early years are now perhaps clouded by an inevitable nostalgia for times past. Deportment and dress were of major concern, as appearances were then of paramount importance. Well-polished footwear, creased trousers, shining buttons, and a well-brushed uniform were demanded. Such priorities were perceived as important for maintaining public respect for the Force. Perhaps understandably in the ever-changing pace of modern life, there is less concern for such concepts. However, it may well be that this lack of concern is damaging to the image of the Force. I have always felt that decent people appreciated seeing well turned-out Gardai patrolling the streets. It was a feeling reinforced by personal contact with the public in all sorts of circumstances, such as at scenes of violence, break-ins, traffic accidents, sudden deaths, and trauma of every kind.

Tours of duty were from 6:00 am to 2:00 pm. and from 2:00 pm to 10:00 pm on alternate days, with the night tour from 10:00 pm to 6:00 am. You were allocated to a particular shift known as a 'relief'. These were for two months on day-duty and one month on night-duty. You stayed with that relief for the rest of your time. The night-relief was always the least attractive option. If you were on the night-relief for December you could expect to spend every Christmas on night-duty. In theory you might expect to spend four months of the year on night-duty – or ten years of your thirty years service.

At the Dún Laoghaire station, as many as nine guards would parade for duty at the commencement of each tour of duty. A sergeant and an inspector visited them on their allotted beats at intervals during their tour. Each man could expect a visit from his sergeant, as well as his inspector, at least once during his tour of duty. Of course, we never knew when to expect a visit. Some sergeants had an uncanny knack of not visiting you until the final hour. Consequently, you were obliged to keep to the rules and not absent yourself from your beat – except for good reason. Such visits were recorded on a beat card and submitted to the Superintendent. The beat cards, giving the time and place of each visit, were carefully scrutinised and an explanation demanded for any inaccuracies or irregularities detected. The Superintendent delegated to a member of his clerical staff the routine daily task of arranging all the beat cards for examination. This checking of the beat cards, like many other aspects of police life in those days, was almost an industry in itself. Indeed, I have often thought that we seemed to spend an inordinate amount of energy and time in simply administering ourselves. It was as if the principles of Parkinson's Law were being applied as a first priority. Not unlike the company shareholders annual meeting giving protracted deliberation to the repair of the staff-bicycle shed at a cost of a hundred euro, while giving instant, unquestioning approval for the purchase of a new atomic reactor.

The men on the beat took the heat with the cold; they asked no questions, but obeyed. Not for them the luxury of special assignments, clerical posts, squad-cars, 'soft jobs', but the leg-weary trudge on the streets of Ireland's towns and cities. At least, in the leafy borough of

Dún Laoghaire-Rathdown, I was lucky enough to have clean streets to trudge and mostly clean-living people on them. But there were moments when the gentility vanished. Most of the time, however, it was dull routine. You were constantly looking at your watch, waiting for your tour to end – and you got very tired. You were looking for action, and there was nothing to do. This very policeman-like activity varied, of course, according to the weather, the time of day and the season of the year.

I started off as a raw recruit in Ringsend, which was then a rough, industrial area. But when you were sent to Sandymount in the other end of the District it was a different world. In those days we went on the beat singly. If you were caught in pairs you might be disciplined, as this was considered a waste of manpower. So you went around like a lone-star ranger, and you didn't have any radio back-up – only a whistle and a baton. You were on your own for whatever contingency might arise. It was lonely, and your thoughts would wander. But, of course, the regulations said you were never to allow anything but your duty to occupy your thoughts. Not an easy thing at four o'clock in the morning. I would be thinking about my holidays, or the girl that I dated last week, or the one I hoped to date next week. You'd be studying the shop windows to keep your mind occupied. There were no screens or shutters in those days, and you got a good view of what was on display. You'd look in and read the covers of the magazines in the newsagents' windows. You had, after all, to keep informed!

On the daytime beat you would look out for traffic offences, which, in hindsight, might seem ridiculous, as there wasn't much traffic in those days. But you would try to attend to your duties and hope something would happen. Before going off duty at night, the checking of premises to make sure they were not broken into was very important, because you might be asked why you had not detected a break-in. This questioning sometimes looked as if authority was trying to justify itself and to be seen doing something – anything. It was almost as if you were the guilty party yourself. On the whole, things were very quiet in those days. Little in the way of major crime would come your way, unless something was reported to you. There were a few corner-boys all right, but they usually moved away as you came along. During a tour of duty an unexpected visit by the Superintendent, or indeed the Chief Superintendent, at an unlikely time or place, would not come as a great surprise.

Patrolling Harbour Road for the arrival of the mail boat was a regular feature of early morning duty at Dún Laoghaire. On one such occasion "Mac" had been allocated this particular duty. He was, by nature, not particularly devoted to high standards of deportment. Indeed, it had been said that he was more comfortable amid agricultural pursuits in his native County Roscommon than patrolling the leafy suburbs of Dún Laoghaire. With his cap set well back on his head, and presenting a benign face to the public at large, Mac was, as you might say, not professionally 'switched on.' With one foot on a low wall and his greatcoat unbuttoned, he awaited the arrival of the 6:30 am mail boat from Holyhead. Oblivious to all around him, he was totally immersed in his morning newspaper, when suddenly from behind he received a sharp tap on the shoulder. Folding his newspaper, while slowly turning around, Mac came face-to-face with the Chief Superintendent. Known as The Razor, the Chief was one of the old brigade – the DMP, which had been absorbed into the Garda Síochána over thirty years before. His sense of propriety would certainly have been of a different order to Mac's. When asked to account for his improper deportment and attention to duty, Mac's laid-back response was, 'To tell you nothing but the truth sir, I wanted to see if a bloke from home was dead'. No doubt, The Razor was unimpressed by Mac's concern for the faithful departed. Disciplinary charges followed, but I am unaware of Mac having been banished to the outer regions of Kerry or Connemara. He served his full term at Dún Laoghaire until he retired to his beloved farm in County Roscommon.

Long before the advent of traffic lights, Pat was the regular traffic man for many years at the top of Marine Road. In truth, he was an ineffectual point-duty man – even in the limited traffic of those days. Wearing his regulation white traffic gloves, Pat would inevitably wave all traffic onwards – while ignoring approaching cross-traffic. In the course of this directing, he habitually turned his back on the traffic that he had just beckoned forward – almost as if to ensure that he was not going to witness a traffic accident. But, as he had been there for many years – almost growing up with the traffic – most locals had come to understand his methods, and few took much notice of his directions – wisely choosing to rely on their own judgment.

However, the story is told that on a certain rare occasion Pat saw fit to reprimand an unfortunate motorist. It seems that the driver, while turning right, had cut in rather sharply behind Pat while his back was turned.

Not at all pleased, Pat exclaimed, "Don't you know that you are supposed to go around me!"

The startled motorist pointed out that Pat was walking away from the centre of the junction and was no longer there.

"It does not matter whether I am there or not – you are supposed to go around me," was Pat's unpredictable but puzzling response.

While standards of deportment and professionalism are essential in a good police force, there is always the need for humanity and commonsense. Much stiffness and official posturing can make life difficult and such behaviour often proves self-defeating. I was always struck by the good response coming from the public whenever we were in a position to be of help. A Garda allowing his natural humanity to surface, and using discretion and commonsense, generated a store of goodwill towards himself personally and towards the Force generally.

This was exemplified on a certain occasion when Mac (yes, that man again) was relieving Pat on his day off. Now, Mac was certainly not the regimental type, and his thoughts and interests did not always revolve around the complications of law enforcement. On this occasion, while he was directing traffic from the centre of the junction, an elderly tourist approached him. The tourist, a low-sized, stout American, in white suit and wide hat, was seeking directions. Mac, a big fellow, placed a large hand on his shoulder and gave detailed directions. I shall never forget the pleased expression on the American's face as he beamed upwards at Mac with a broad smile spread on his face. They engaged in prolonged, jovial conversion, as the traffic obligingly ignored them both. I thought of Percy French's hero, Peter O'Loughlin, who, "stopped the whole street with one wave of his hand, while the whole population of London looked on."

On rare occasions, one became embroiled in the tragic side of life. One day I came face to face with a suicide. It was 2:00 pm, and we had just come on duty. I was directed by Sergeant John to accompany him to a house from which a call for help had been received earlier in the day. We were not quite sure of the nature of the call. Others had been kicking-to-touch until we came on duty, to avoid becoming involved. Of course, one came across this sort of thing from time to time. The Sergeant, not an over-confident man, to say the least, ushered me in before him as we were admitted to the house. "You go first," was his instruction when we were directed towards the kitchen. On squeezing through the slightly blocked half-open kitchen door I found a man stretched on the floor with his head on a pillow in the gas oven. He was very obviously dead. When the Sergeant eventually and slowly put his head around the kitchen door, I said to him, "We've got a problem here, Sergeant." He looked aghast at me and, quite startled, nervously stammered, "But, but, this man is dead." It was a problem for him.

On another occasion I took a young recruit out on the beat on his very first day. I had left him alone for a few minutes near the public toilets when the toilet attendant drew his attention to some indecency inside – some buggery going on. The young recruit was confronted with an unusual and rather difficult case on his very first hours on duty. He had to make an arrest, of course. In forty years I had never to make such an arrest. But that's the kind of thing you could walk into at any time.

I was never involved in a riot, and I never felt obliged to hit anyone with a baton during all my years in the Force. But I know that colleagues of mine had sometimes to do so. That sort of thing is all in the lap of the gods. The nearest I came to such a confrontation was in 1945 on V-J day, that is Victory in Japan day. There was a lot of celebration and drunkenness on the streets. Two hooligans were fighting each other down on the tram tracks in Lower George's Street right in front of me. Of course, there was no way that the law could stand idly by. However, when I stepped down from the footpath, calling on them to stop, they immediately joined forces and turned on me. As is often the case, the face of authority at once became the common enemy. Fortunately, before blows were struck, a colleague, Harry, on plain-clothes duty nearby, sailed in with his mighty fists. Just two blows were struck, our two heroes were on their backs, and that was the end of the matter. I'm told you can't do that sort of thing anymore.

A colleague and I arrested a man one day for unruly behaviour. We needed to bring him to the station about a mile away. We had no car. We had no radio either. We tried to put the fellow on a tram. We had no handcuffs. We had nothing. He was a very strong man and much the worse for drink. He held the centre rail in a vice-like grip and refused to move forward into the tram. We struggled, barehanded, for five minutes before we managed to break his grip. All of this on Dublin's public transport system, with the conductor and passengers watching in nervous apprehension. As I said, we had no handcuffs. These were always at the station – three or four pairs of them. I doubt if I saw them used once.

The Dublin Division of the Garda Síochána, to which I was allocated in 1944, was modelled on the pattern of the DMP of the previous century. The name had changed, but not much else. You could be disciplined for gossiping on the beat. Now, that could be with a colleague or with a member of the public. At the same time, you were supposed to encourage conversation and get to know the people. You were often told to use your own discretion when you sought directions from your superiors. This was really a cop-out, as they were not prepared to give you a firm, clear-cut instruction in a particular situation. Hence the term 'Use your own discretion' became something of a joke in the Force. Twomey had been assigned to special indoor duty for many years and part of his duty was the delivery of internal mail to Dublin Castle. He seldom wore the uniform. When asked by the new Superintendent why he was not in uniform, he replied, "I always used my own discretion, sir." Quickly came the direction: "In future you will use my discretion and wear a uniform!"

But on the whole, we did use our own discretion, and we talked to most people. What kind of people would talk to me though, that was another question? And what kind of people should I talk to? You would not talk to everybody –you would not talk to corner-boys. Some people would be very glad to talk to you, or pleased if you talked to them. I was always aware of that. There was great respect for the law. A certain type of person would bring you into their homes and welcome you. It was always a source of pride to know that you were trusted and respected because you were a Garda.

At five o'clock one morning, a milkman knocked on the station door. "I've something here for you," he said. I had no idea what he meant. Stepping outside I was soon to find out. Slumped across his horse-drawn milk dray was a bespectacled middle-aged man. Huddled up in a duffel coat and looking very drunk, he was in fact badly drugged. The milkman had found him on his hands and knees in the middle of the road up in Killiney. We got the guy into the station and sitting in a chair, but could not get his name – as he was doped 'to the eyeballs.' It was my very first experience of the drug scene. This was in the early 1950s, long before the drug epidemic came to Ireland. We discovered later the poor man had been through a love affair that went wrong. This morning he had come from England, got off the mail-boat at Dún Laoghaire, gone up to Killiney Hill and taken an overdose of tablets. When he was found he had several sealed envelopes attached to the buttonholes in his duffel coat. He had come prepared with these envelopes addressed to various people in England. One envelope addressed to "Jane" had £250 marked on the outside, but when opened it contained £500.

Sergeant John was aghast. He was, as I have already related, a nervous man, and the very last thing he wished for at this hour of the morning was a drug addict. When recording details of the matter, the Sergeant ended his report with the words: "The property was taken possession of by Garda Gunn." Of course I shouldn't have taken possession of it. That was his job, and it should have been left at the station. But he wasn't going to risk leaving it there, because he was thinking of the possibility, however remote, that it might get mislaid. The Sergeant had made it quite clear that he wasn't going to take charge of it. I had to bring the money home with me. It was all very irregular, but probably the wisest thing to do. At least I could ensure that it found its way to the safe in the Superintendent's office.

Sergeant John was normally on outdoor duty, which allowed him to 'get lost' if he so desired. Occasionally he was obliged to take up relief duty in the office. Now this was not what he wanted at all, as here he was confined and forced to accept responsibility for anything that turned up. Needless to say, he was constantly praying that his tour would end without having to face a major, or indeed any, incident. Having completed his tour of office duty without incident, he'd emerge from the office with a broad smile on his normally worried face, and joyfully rubbing his hands with great relief he'd cheerfully exclaim, "Oh boys, oh boys! That's another day done.' He was another day nearer his pension.

Chapter 18

No Home from Home

My years at Dalkey were happy years and I was contented to let life take its course. It was 1954 when the authority ordained that I should transfer to Dún Laoghhaire, two miles down the road. Although happy to remain in Dalkey, I did not regard the change as of any great inconvenience as I was then no longer living in the station.

Now the standards of accommodation provided in most Garda stations at that time were very basic indeed. Furnishings were minimal, and many of the stations were in fact buildings that had been converted from their original purpose. However, standards at Dún Laoghaire would have been regarded as somewhat above average, and, having regard to its history, this is perhaps not surprising because it was originally built as a convent.

The history of the old convent had a certain fascination for me. In 1827 the Order of Poor Clare nuns established a convent at 100 Upper George's Street, and it became known as Kingstown Convent, until the nuns returned to Dublin in 1834. It was sold to the Police Authority for £1150 on 4th December 1839, and occupied by the DMP in 1840. And so, the convent building, which had echoed to Matins and Evensong, was destined to become home to generations of police from 1840 until its closure in 1992. The chapel, rooms, and living quarters of the Poor Clare nuns became offices, day-rooms, parade-rooms, living quarters and so on. They would remain so for over 150 years, and few would have realised that for over 150 years the doors of this building never closed.

One day in 1992 word reached me that the station, by then vacated, was being demolished. Camcorder in hand, I hurried to capture the dying moments of the old building that had such a unique history. I stood there amidst the swirling dust and noise as the walls came tumbling down, and reflected on history disappearing before my very eyes. The building now being laid low had been host to holy and gentle nuns, generations of stern and caring policemen – and at times to miscreants, rogues, thieves and beggars. As the wrecking ball did its work and roofs crumbled, I thought, if those stones could only talk what stories would unfold

Over the years, the building had been adapted internally, in an attempt to meet the needs of changing times – not with much success, it has to be said. In the main, it remained much the same as when first built in 1827. Its three and four stories comprised small rooms and narrow corridors, and these were accessed by a very impressive central stairway, having a fine mahogany balustrade that remained in excellent condition until the very end. The original chapel ceiling remained untouched and survived until the final days.

And so it was that this old convent building, which had served both church and state, came to a sudden – almost violent end. As the bulldozer wrote the final chapter and the demolition men carted away the bricks and mortar, I almost sensed the spirits of other days gather in silent, sad dissent. Whenever I pass the Post Office that replaced the old building at 100 Upper George's Street, I pause and think of the convent that became a police station. Perhaps, too, I sometimes fantasize – and listen for the distant sound of marching feet in search of a last farewell.

As well as being the principal centre of police administration, the building had also been home to generations of young, and the not so young, members of the Force. In those days it was obligatory for all unmarried members of the Force to reside in stations. Over thirty members would have resided there at any one time. Meals were provided from a large kitchen on the ground floor. A staff of cooks, cleaners, yardman and a messenger boy was employed there. Expenses were defrayed from a common fund to which all were obliged to contribute.

In the early days, two very fine lithograph prints of Arthur Griffith and General Michael Collins featured in nearly every Garda station. A pair of these prints hung on either side of the fireplace in the large mess-room at Dún Laoghaire. They had been there for many years, but, sad to say, they became somewhat neglected, as the idealism which had inspired their installation diminished with the passing years. Some years before retirement, my colleague, Jim Crowley, and I seized the opportunity of having them restored. Both pictures were later, on our retirement, placed in the safety of the District Stores. Another feature was a picture of the Sacred Heart to commemorate the Holy Year of 1950. Purchased by members living in the station at the time, it hung for many years in the corner of the mess room, constantly illuminated by a little oil lamp.

With its large open fireplace and long dining table, the mess-room was at the heart of life in the station. Here everyone met, not only for meals but also when going on and off duty. At night-time, before the age of television, it was a place for telling stories and playing cards. An annual Mass for deceased members was usually held on the 6th January and was always very well attended. At Christmas there was a party to which many friends and associates were invited. Johnny Doran, a colourful yardman-cum-messenger, was also something of an actor. Johnny usually entertained all present by dressing up and performing in drag. Bridie Bennett, a much-loved cook for many years, excelled at dispensing hospitality on these social occasions. It was in many ways one of the few public-relations opportunities open to us in those days. Bridie was something of a mother figure to many of the younger members of the Force. She had seen them come and go – sometimes marry and sometimes die.

There was, however, a gloomy side to life in the station. Like most buildings of the period, it was difficult to heat. It had no central heating; ventilation was poor, and it was frugally furnished, as only the basic necessities were supplied. A crisis was eventually reached when the Gardai, who had been protesting at the increasingly dangerous condition of the building, threatened to walk out unless something was done soon. It was demolished on 17th October 1992, after it had been vacated and the Gardaí had moved to a new purpose-built station at Corrig Avenue.

Directly opposite the old Garda Station was Courtney's wholesale tobacco shop on Upper George's Street. P.J. Courtney & Son had traded there for many years and were very well known in the town. Little did we expect that one day soon those premises would become part of the most intricate case ever to appear on our books.

In the 1950s, a large advertisement appeared in the *Irish Times,* proclaiming the possibility of making a large profit with complete security from an investment of as little as £10. This advert was the initial step by one Paul Singer, who had infiltrated the long-established second-hand furniture business known as Shanahan's Furniture Auctions.

Who was this man who had devised a plan to make money without any risk? He was not taking risks with his own money, but with investors' money. 'Doctor' Singer, as he liked to style himself, was an East European Jew who came to Ireland in 1954. He was a big, suave man, like a character from an old world movie. He wore dark horn-rimmed spectacles and had a goatee beard and moustache. Invariably dressed in a black pin-striped suit, he was a larger-than-life character who exuded confidence and was always very much in command. He was so impressive that those who met him were unlikely to forget him.

Now, Singer had a brainwave. Dublin could become the capital of world philately. To this end he engaged the interests of Jerome Shanahan who ran a small second-hand furniture business in Dún Laoghaire. Shanahan was an honest Kerryman who had fought in the First World War. He had been holding weekly furniture auctions in an old Mission Hall premises at Corrig Avenue in the heart of Dún Laoghaire for many years when Singer arrived. The suave Singer engaged Jerome with his proposition for the setting up of a stamp auction business in his premises.

At the time, when things were going very well for the new venture, I recall asking Jerome Shanahan how he first became involved with the 'Doctor,' as he insisted on calling Singer. "He just walked in off the street and put the proposition to me, and I thought why not have a go," was his reply.

Jerome's son Desmond had just qualified as a solicitor, and he, his wife and father became directors of Shanahan's Stamp Auctions, along with Paul Singer and his wife Erma. An advertising blitz was launched in the media and circulars sent to collectors and dealers all over Ireland and abroad. Profits as high as forty percent on investments were promised and a broad spectrum of society was surprisingly quick to respond to this unusual opportunity to make easy money. There were, of course, many who wondered sceptically about the possibilities of making money by just buying and selling postage stamps.

Nevertheless, 'Doctor' Paul Singer had acquired all the outward signs of success by securing a stake in Shanahan's long-established business. Indeed, one of my own senior colleagues, who had now reached retirement age, decided to retire when given the opportunity of joining 'Doctor' Singer's team. Seemingly nothing could go wrong with this ground-breaking scheme. Reports of huge profits spread like wildfire, and investments poured into Singer's coffers. The more money that came in, the more he could expand the whole enterprise. On this rising tide of success Singer secured prestigious offices directly opposite the Garda Station on Dún Laoghaire's high street. He also opened offices adjoining the splendid Adelphi Cinema premises further up the street.

Publicity and a high-profile image were essential if the venture was to succeed, and Singer - never a man to do things by half - launched his stamp auction with great publicity and aplomb. Champagne parties and press interviews were the order of the day. I recall one particular anniversary party which he hosted at Coring Avenue. Edmundo Ross's famous rumba band was flown over from London to entertain guests at the Corrig Avenue premises into the small hours of the morning. Wine flowed all night, as the rapturous sounds of one of the world's most popular dance bands echoed through the Victorian alleyways of old Dún Laoghaire. 'The Doctor' had indeed established himself as a man-about-town, while making a fortune and throwing the best party ever held in the Borough of Dún Laoghaire.

Alas, the chickens were about to come to roost, and soon the party would be over. Investments were unable to sustain the advertised high profits which were so necessary for the continued success of the scheme. What might be described as the chain-letter aspect of the scheme raised its ugly head. In May 1959 the bubble burst, with Singer claiming it collapsed on account of an alleged break-in at the Adelphi offices and the theft of his most recent purchase – the valuable Burrus Collection.

The Fraud Squad was called in and lots of documents were impounded. A special office to deal with the case was set up at the Garda station and investigations went on for about two years, until a prosecution was initiated. The Shanahans and Singer were arrested. The Shanahans got bail but Singer was unable to provide the necessary security and was detained in Mountjoy Jail. While there, he demanded the right of access to law books in order to conduct his own defence. He was afforded the use of an extra cell for the storage of such books, and studied the law intensely while in custody, pending his appeal to the High Court. Following protracted court proceedings over many months, Singer was sentenced to 14 years imprisonment. However, the very clever 'Doctor' Singer was not to be defeated. He appealed the sentence, and after a period of nearly three years his sentence was eventually quashed – case not proven.

The other defendants were less fortunate. Desmond Shanahan and his wife went to England, and Jerome, although continuing to live in Dún Laoghaire, vanished from the public eye. There would be no more stamp auctions, nor indeed, furniture auctions.

Paul Singer always played it big. Publicity and a high profile status were the hallmarks of his successes. He took large advertising space in the *Irish Times*, thereby giving respectability and assurance to his public image. Singer asserted himself as the biggest player in the philatelic world and claimed to have purchased in Switzerland the most comprehensive and valuable stamp collection in the world. Although without legal qualification, he was more than a match for the leading lawyers and ably defended himself in a £1m fraud case, and is known to have advised other prisoners on how best to prepare their defence.

Singer always claimed that his stamp auction scheme was legitimate, and were it not for the break-in and the larceny of the Burrus collection, Shanahan's Stamp Auctions would have proven an undoubted success. In any event 'Doctor' Singer, sometimes referred to as 'The Doctor of

Millions', walked away a free man and settled in Canada, never to return to Ireland.

The liquidator of Shanahan's Stamp Auctions sent a telegram to Singer in Canada requesting some assistance in the liquidation process. Singer replied that he would like to travel to Ireland to assist the bankruptcy proceedings, but was unable to do so, on account of his mother's illness. Several sightings of Singer in different locations were reported from time to time. I understand that he eventually died in Canada.

For many years after his departure, Singer's legacy left a lasting scar on Irish society. It had exposed the latent greed inherent in human nature, and that many are unable to resist the temptation to amass great riches.

Chapter 19

Beyond the Call of Duty

I was – like those who went before me – soon to experience the realities of life, to learn that answers to every problem were not to be found in the pages of the law books or the mountain of rules and regulations which governed daily life in the Force. Answers were more likely to be found in the hard school of experience. The varied nature of our daily tasks was such that the use of common sense and discretion was essential. We learned that answers were not always cast in stone, and a certain maturity took hold before we knew it.

My youthful concepts of marital bliss were sometimes diminished by early experiences. Domestic quarrels between husband and wife are well-documented in police stations. Calls for intervention usually came from the same source. The more senior men knew the 'regulars' by heart and consequently, were well seasoned in their approach to such calls.

When first sent on such a mission, I recall my sense of dismay that mature married people could cause such distress to each other. It so happened that there was no violence involved in my first case, and I later came to realise that such non-violent squabbles were quite a frequent occurrence. Stephen was a decent man, tidy and well-dressed, who kept a lovely garden, but occasionally 'went on the batter' when his monthly pension cheque arrived. His good wife would phone the Garda station, as the occasion demanded and - in true police tradition - a man would be sent. My first visit to the normally impeccable Stephen, now unshaven, barefoot and dishevelled, in verbal confrontation with his portly wife, was a sight to behold. In a colourful, flowing dressing gown, fancy slippers and hair-curlers, the angry woman paced the untidy bedroom. A partially-used chamber pot was clearly visible under the bed, and an array of bedclothes and wearing apparel were scattered throughout the room. It was a scene that did little for my youthful, idealistic concept of married life.

Such an experience would be repeated many times over the coming years – and often required much firmer intervention than the talk I gave to Stephen. Happily, peace was restored and, as was usually the case, no charges were preferred. Stephen and his wife were reconciled – until next pension day. Indeed, the role of the Force in the many trials and tribulations of domestic life is, perhaps, not quite fully appreciated by society. There are many personal acts of kindness, well beyond the call of duty, performed by individual members that go unrecorded and unsung, which are taken for granted by a society that has really never experienced the tyranny of extreme officialdom.

On the other hand, it was my own happy experience to encounter the genuine appreciation often shown for the simplest service – official or otherwise. Indeed, I feel that it has been a privilege to be placed in a position to serve those in need of help in whatever form. This is illustrated by a simple incident in 1946. A young girl, who had travelled up from the country, was trying to locate her uncle's house in one of the more modest dwellings in the area. She had taken the last tram from Dublin, was unclear about her uncle's address, and was quite lost in the darkness of the night. Despite the lateness of the hour, I managed to locate the house. The grateful old man, of modest enough means, was insisting, firstly, that I should partake of a bottle of stout. When this was politely refused, tea was offered. Again, I felt obliged to decline. However, not to be outdone, and unknown to me, he had furtively slipped a small packet of cigarettes into my greatcoat pocket as I squeezed through the narrow doorway on leaving.

The entire episode was laced with profound expressions of thanks and gratitude for having delivered his little niece to the safety of his humble home. Any feeling of satisfaction I experienced was enhanced by a realization of the extent to which the man appreciated the little I had done. Of course, by its very nature, the role of the police is often perceived as being primarily centred on law enforcement. But the social role of the Force should not be overlooked. Many years ago, the late

Archbishop McQuaid, when opening a Garda-sponsored youth club in Finglas, expressed the opinion that there should be a greater role for the Garda Síochána in this regard.

As in the case of Willie Birmingham of ALONE fame[*] the Garda, by the very nature of his job, is brought into contact with people whose difficult circumstances often lie hidden and unknown. A desire to provide help and comfort was frequently met by the twin obstacles of bureaucracy and apathy, and, no doubt, there are countless examples of such experiences. My own recollections of such situations are best highlighted by an experience I had in my final years of service. There had been a huge increase in the size, as well as in the ubiquity of housing estates. The quality of housing had improved beyond all recognition, and the inherited slums of past decades were fast becoming a bad memory. At 4 o'clock one cold winter afternoon as I approached the house of my assignment, I was immediately struck by the unkempt state of the obviously once-pretty garden. Artistic wrought-iron work lay broken and rusting amid rank weeds in the unkempt flowerbeds. Hardboard replaced the broken glass in the hall-door. A tattered lace curtain flapped despondently in an adjoining broken window, and I had an ominous premonition that all was not well.

I had come to investigate the poor school attendance record of a member of the household. Following my repeated knocking, the door was eventually opened by a rather dishevelled, pale-faced boy, who, although fully dressed, had obviously just got out of bed. He was about twelve years of age, of delicate build and sad visage. Although the weather was cold and wintry, the house was unheated, and I could feel the chill in the atmosphere. Glancing over the boy's shoulder, I became aware of the kitchen, which was in an appalling state of filth and disarray. Decayed, uneaten food, empty whiskey bottles and broken furniture were scattered around the floor. Worse was to be revealed. On

---

[*] Willie Bermingham was a fireman in Dublin. In his work Willie frequently came across abandoned and neglected old people living in squalid conditions. After seeing the plight of the elderly, he set up ALONE which stands for *A Little Offering Never Ends*.

entering the rear garden, through a creaky open doorway, I was confronted by a mountain of black refuse bags which had obviously been piling up over a long period of time. Worst of all was the blocked sewerage pipe, which had burst and was seeping halfway up the garden, turning it into a quagmire. I could hardly believe my eyes! That such conditions should prevail in a perfectly good house, the property of the Local Authority, was beyond belief.

On further investigation, I learned that these conditions had been a cause of great concern to the neighbours. The facts had been reported to the Local Authority and the Health Board, and apparently nothing had been done. Although what I was witnessing was not within my remit, I felt, for what it was worth, that further action on my part was called for.

In the following days, I made a report directly to the responsible medical officer, Dr. Quinn, who, I am very glad to say took immediate action. This involved convening a meeting of social workers, health inspectors, district nursing staff and housing officers, under the auspices of Dr. Quinn, the Community Health Officer. It appears that while the house in question had been occasionally visited over a period of time by health inspectors, social workers and local housing officials, nothing had been done.

The system had failed a young family, which had fallen on bad times through unforeseen economic circumstances, occasioned by an international oil crisis at the time. The father ran a small metal-fabricating business, which depended heavily on orders for central-heating oil tanks. When the demand ceased, he got into serious financial difficulties and unfortunately turned to alcohol. Both he and his wife grossly neglected their home, and seemed to loose all sense of responsibility. The three young boys were more or less left to fend for themselves. As a result of the Community Health Officer's action, the case was eventually monitored and steps taken to provide for the future health and housing needs of the family. It is with much pleasure that I recall the support and positive role of other members of the community in this case. A detective colleague approached the manager of a local hotel, who willingly employed one of the boys as a porter – on condition that he opened a Post Office Savings Account and went to night school.

This boy subsequently won promotion in the hotel and went on to develop a fine career in the catering industry.

There was also the role of a local charity committee, which arranged for the 'winning' of a Christmas hamper by the family in question, in order to help them over a difficult period. The headmaster of the school concerned took a deep interest in the case. He confided to me that all three boys were of university calibre and, were it not for their unfortunate circumstances, would surely have gone on to higher things. I had no reason to doubt his judgment. I was fortunate, also, in having contacted a helpful local priest, whose encouragement and support was invaluable. The family recovered completely from the trauma that had befallen them – thanks to a diligent Community Health Officer and those caring individuals whom I had the good fortune to meet. In my twilight years, I find much satisfaction in recalling the happy resolution of this episode.

Chapter 20

Sudden Death – Tricky Situations

The duties of An Garda Síochána are wide and varied, even if mostly routine. This was especially so in the quiet suburbs of Dalkey and Killiney. However, you never could tell what might turn up, or where exactly you might be.

Sudden deaths were a case in point. These were invariably tinged with sadness, especially when the deceased was elderly and lived alone. One day, when directed to a little house on Coliemore Road in Dalkey, I had my first experience of this. Miss McCullagh was an old lady who lived in one of the many little gate lodges, which were a feature of the area. These were usually very simple two-roomed stone dwellings built within the grounds of a big house for the use of a gardener or domestic employee. With the passage of time and with changing economic circumstances, these little lodges frequently became a source of revenue to supplement the owner's income. Retired unmarried ladies of limited means and with few family connections were usually regarded as desirable tenants. They sought only to live out their final years as best they could in peaceful tranquillity. Miss McCullagh was one of them.

It was a lovely morning in early summer. As I entered the little house I was at once aware of an uncanny stillness. The sun's rays flickered through the old-fashioned lace curtains onto the windowsill where a potted geranium spread its blooms. A small landscape painting and two little china dogs held pride of place on an otherwise empty mantelpiece. The principal furniture consisted of two hardback chairs, a plain wooden table, a small sideboard and a little cane table beside the single iron bed in the corner opposite the front door. A well-worn hearthrug was the sole concession to luxury in the frugally furnished bedroom.

My most vivid recollection is of the little iron bed and the very still form of Miss McCullagh reposing in apparent serenity. From her facial expression I could see that she must have died quite peacefully. She had a smile on her beautiful face, as if she had been welcoming a long lost friend. Dressed in a spotlessly clean nightdress, she lay motionless on the snow-white sheets. Her eyes were closed, her delicate hands clasping a small partly-open Bible, and I felt that the good Lord may have come to visit this dear lady. Perhaps that was the explanation for her welcoming smile.

There were several cases of a somewhat similar nature during my years of service. These were blandly referred to as 'a sudden death', and a subject for routine official investigation. Around each such death there was an inevitable touch of emotion, but after sixty years my memory of Miss McCullagh's final hours still remains as fresh as if it were yesterday.

Of course, one was really never too far away from scenes of death. It invariably horrified me to have to stand idly by at the scene of a serious accident and watch helplessly as somebody struggled for life. I am reminded here of one such accident at Rock Road in Booterstown. A passing truck struck a handsome young boy aged about thirteen years as he stepped off the footpath. We were called to the scene, but there was nothing we could do to save the young boy's life. As he lay unconscious on the footpath, I could see a trickle of blood slowly seep from his ear, and I knew that his condition was grave. A passing doctor advised me not to attempt first-aid. The ambulance eventually arrived, and by this time I had ascertained the boy's address, which was in the locality.

I called to inform his relatives. A heavily pregnant woman, the boy's mother, opened the door in response to my knock. What was I to do? When a policeman calls to someone's door uninvited, it is usually not a good omen. You can detect the apprehension in most people's eyes. The best I could come up with was to say that a slight accident had occurred and, that her son had been taken to hospital as a precaution. In my heart I felt sure that never again would this good woman see her son alive – and so it was.

Unfortunately, fatal traffic accidents on Rock Road were all too common. The causes were sometimes freakish and unbelievably bizarre.

Arriving at the aftermath of one such accident, I stood aghast at the scene before me. A rather dilapidated old lorry had crashed into an ESB lamp post and three men were trapped inside. All three were sitting upright. The driver sat fully conscious but in a state of shock behind the wheel, and on the bench seat sat two other men. The man next to the driver was alive and clearly in a state of shock, while the third man was dead. He was the only one of the three who had received any injuries.

The cause of this accident was, as I have said, bizarre. The old lorry carried a load of farm-manure, and when a motorist travelling immediately in front of the lorry failed to give a right-hand signal the lorry driver was obliged to swerve suddenly to his left to avoid a collision. As a result of this manoeuvre, the load of farm-manure shifted and threw the lorry out of control. It crashed violently into the lamp-post and the unfortunate man on the left received the full impact. There he was, badly cut from top to bottom, embedded in the lamp-post, and clearly dead. The two survivors were unable to speak, and it was some time before the rescue services were able to free them from the wrecked lorry.

Calling to people's hall-doors to give notification of a serious accident or death was always difficult and traumatic. It was a dreaded task and one which had to be handled with great sensitivity, depending on the circumstances and the relationship of the deceased to the person opening the door.

One night, about 12 o'clock, we got a call from Co Wicklow asking us to inform the relatives of a local man that he had died in a traffic accident. A commercial traveller, he returned regularly to his wife in Dalkey every Friday night from his travels throughout the country. On this occasion he had been driving home from Wicklow when he became the victim of a fatal heart attack, and died on the roadside.

He and his wife had been living in an apartment on the top floor of a very tall terraced house. My instructions were to 'inform the relatives' but, of course, I had no idea who they might be. I rang the door-bell at 12:30 am and wondered who might appear. Eventually, the deceased's wife opened the door, and I could see that she was surprised to find a policeman standing there. Wondering how she might react to the bad news, I thought seriously about how I would phrase my message. How on earth do you impart that sort of information to an unprepared and unsuspecting person? Aware that she lived alone on the very top floor, I was anxious to guard against unforeseen difficulties, such as a fainting fit, or a hysterical reaction. So, before breaking the news I suggested that, as the night was cold, she might like to go inside before we discussed the purpose of my visit. She was by now quite apprehensive and insisted on being told immediately. I hesitantly referred to a serious traffic accident.

"How serious?" was her next question?

"Very serious – with loss of life," was my response.

Her reaction was one of stoic calm. I was amazed at her quiet self-control when I confirmed that her husband had died. After a few silent minutes, I offered to accompany her to her apartment upstairs and as we climbed several flights of stairs I pondered if there was anything further I could do to help.

The tragedy of the occasion was accentuated by the homeliness of the cosy living room. The table was set for two, and despite the lateness of the night, a lively coal-fire burned brightly in the old-fashioned fireplace, while nearby a pair of gent's slippers sadly awaited the owner's return. The sudden unforeseen and cruel disruption to the lives of those concerned was pathetically obvious.

I offered sympathetic words. How could I be of help? Was there some relative or friend I could contact? However, nothing it seemed was practical at that late hour, and I was thanked for the consideration. She would be all right, would go to bed and deal with matters in the morning. Again I marvelled at her calmness and thought deeply of the days and nights she was now forced to spend alone and uncomforted. With my knock on the door her life had been changed – changed utterly.

On another occasion, while on patrol car duty on the Merrion Road, a stark message came over the car radio: "Car 8, go to Killiney where an aeroplane has fallen into the sea." Nothing more than that – a very simple instruction you might say. But I had no idea at all what was involved. My first thoughts were of an Are Lingus Boeing having crashed with a loss of hundreds of lives.

It was August and we were having one of those rare, fine summers. The weather had been very warm for weeks, and crowds were flocking to the beaches. As quickly as possible we made the journey through the dense holiday traffic to Killiney, where the beach was packed with day-trippers. On arrival, I was at once aware of the crowd of onlookers near the water's edge. They were agog at the sight of an elderly, very distressed woman attempting to wade seawards in the shallow waters to reach a small aeroplane which was half submerged some hundred yards off shore.

The small biplane had apparently got into difficulties while flying over Killiney Bay and had crash-landed into the sea, killing both occupants. I discovered that one of the victims was this poor woman's only son. She presented a most pitiful sight: up to her waist in water and overwhelmed with grief, while the distressing scene was sullied by the presence of a swarm of onlookers. I was incensed at the distasteful spectacle of the gaping crowd insensitively staring at this broken-hearted mother whose distress, so clearly obvious to all, was being turned into a gigantic open-air peepshow.

Feeling deeply for the unfortunate woman, I appealed to the faceless crowd to show some compassion and disperse. I firmly escorted her out of the water and back to the waiting police car so that she might be spared the trauma of seeing her son's body being taken from the sea. Sometimes you were torn between the importance of doing your duty and a dread of being unkind or officious!

There was the occasion when I had a 'brush with the cloth.' It was 3:00 am when an erratically-driven car attracted my attention. When I succeeded in stopping the car, I found the driver, a rural parish priest, quite intoxicated and unfit to drive. Now, I have to say that I was not particularly keen on arresting clergymen or anybody else, if that could be avoided. The situation presented me with a dilemma, as there was no way that I could allow him to continue on his journey. I could visualise the outcome if I affected an arrest: the good priest would be detained until sober and then charged to appear in court the next day. This was not a scenario that appealed to me. I reasoned that in this case, because no harm had been done and no complaints made, justice would not be best served by making an arrest. I took control of the car and drove his reverence to his temporary address at Ballsbridge. Here I took his house key, let him in the front door and put his keys into the letterbox. I then returned on foot to Dún Laoghaire, feeling that I had done the right thing.

Chapter 21

Meeting an Archbishop

By the time I had completed twelve years' service, I was increasingly aware of the many shortcomings and seemingly unnecessary frustrations of daily life in the Garda Síochána. It was routine procedure for the inspecting officer to invite us to voice any complaints we may have had. It was unheard-of that such a call would elicit a response and it was an invitation no-one took seriously – except me. I may have been naive in believing that something useful might be achieved by raising simple issues, such as working conditions, and perhaps I was only making a pointless charade not intended to be taken seriously. Now 'a little sincerity can be a dangerous thing,' and an unlikely outcome of my mischief-making led to unforeseen consequences.

On one of those dull, wintry days early in 1956, as I was going off duty at Dún Laoghaire, a colleague, Edward Brady, approached me with the suggestion that I should allow my name to go forward as a candidate in the forthcoming elections to the Garda Representative Bodies. Now, thoughts of such matters were very far from my mind. Like most of my colleagues, I had little awareness of the Garda Representative Bodies. The image and profile of that organization was such that there was no great rush of applicants for the honour of becoming a District Representative and there was general indifference at grassroots level.

My only credentials appear to have been that, in the course of monthly inspections, I had drawn attention to some of the more archaic regulations governing our lives. All of this is a long way from my early reminiscences of Manorhamilton, Pomeroy, and my first years in the Force. During those early years we were not overly interested in serious issues. The term *industrial relations* was unknown to most of us, we had more exciting things to occupy our thoughts – girlfriends, the lads, football glories and so on. We were fortunate enough to have a job and the future could be left to posterity.

It was no wonder, then, that there was little interest in the Representative Bodies; all that sort of thing could be left to others. But I recall my mixed feelings while on duty at Dún Laoghaire pier as I watched the queues of emigrants. After Christmas was always the worst time – the weather was usually miserable and there was that 'hung-over' feeling. The packed train from Westland Row disgorged the unhappy travellers onto the pier, where a rather indifferent British Rail management unceremoniously ushered them up the gangway. Depending on the tides, the gangway was sometimes tilted at a precarious angle that demanded the skill of a trapeze artist. The discourteous instructions, often robustly voiced by a seemingly uncaring management, left a lot to be desired. In the words of Pat Rabbitte[*], "it was a time of equality of scarcity." As I walked away and the departing mail-boat steamed out of the harbour, I usually had a feeling of sadness for those forced to emigrate – and I with my permanent, secure job here in Ireland. I almost felt guilty.

But, permanent and secure as my job was, it was not without its downside. As we grow older we become more analytical – even critical. I gradually became aware of many irritating and archaic regulations, which seemed totally irrelevant. Likewise, there were unnecessary shortcomings, as well as unjustifiable aspects of the disciplinary code. Some of my colleagues had similar thoughts, and we frequently discussed such matters. Eventually, I was drawn into the field of industrial relations in the Garda Síochána in the late 1950s.

My memories of the past invariably lead me to recollections of that involvement. Suffice for now to reflect on that brief period when I found myself cast in a role that I had not anticipated or envisaged. It was

---

[*] TD for Dublin South West. Formerly Minister of State at the Department of Enterprise, Trade and Employment with responsibility for Commerce, Science and Technology.

highlighted by involvement with the problems of a new generation of Guards, and with such luminaries as the Archbishop of Dublin, John Charles McQuaid, Justice Minister Charles J. Haughey, Economist Garrett Fitzgerald, and others. I reflect on our idealism of the time, as we sought to establish a truly creditable representative body.

My first meeting with the Archbishop McQuaid, was on the occasion of the opening of the Dominic Savio Boys Club in Dublin in 1959. As secretary of the Representative Body for Guards, I had sent a personal contribution through those Gardaí who had founded the club. Dr.McQuaid had been invited to officiate at the blessing of the club premises in Finglas, and I received an invitation to attend the formal opening ceremony. I recall his observation to me that evening: "The Garda Síochána could play a greater role in the social life of the community." His observation was somewhat far-seeing, as in those distant days the role of the Force was not officially perceived in such idealistic terms. It is to the credit of those particular men of the Garda Síochána who, without official support or encouragement, pioneered such a role for themselves. Thankfully, there has since been a great reversal in official attitudes - with worthwhile programmes launched in support of youth clubs and local communities.

Two years later I met the Archbishop in much more dramatic circumstances. It was late, very late, on a cold November night in 1961 when we arrived at the Archbishop's residence in Killiney, County Dublin. As Secretary of the Representative Body for Guards I had been invited with others to meet the Archbishop. We had driven out from the Dublin Institute of Catholic Sociology in Eccles Street with Father Fehily, Director of the Institute. The meeting had been hastily arranged at the Archbishop's request, as he wished to mediate in a serious disciplinary crisis which was plaguing the Garda Síochána. The crisis had arisen as a result of dissatisfaction with a recent pay award, and unauthorized protest meetings which led to the dismissal of eleven young Gardaí who had been protesting their exclusion from the pay award.

As Father Fehily's car swung through the magnificent iron gateway and up the dark, leafy driveway, I pondered the possibilities of this unusual nocturnal meeting. The long avenue led to a wide open sweep in front of the Archbishop's house, where we were about to meet one of the most powerful men in Ireland.

On entering through the high double front door into an oak-panelled hallway, we were shown into a magnificent inner hall. This luxurious Victorian Gothic redbrick mansion, standing in several acres of woodland, was built in the mid-1800s. The high ceilings of the spacious rooms, with beautiful cornices of egg and dart mouldings, breathed a magnificence far removed from the Garda stations of the day.

I had not been in an archbishop's palace before, and the occasion was somewhat overwhelming. It was dramatized by the nature of our mission, the urgency with which we had been brought there, and the unsociable hour of the meeting. We were ushered into a large, comfortable room, where a glowing coal-fire spread its heat from the depths of an impressive marble fireplace. The solid period furniture, the heavy tapestry curtains, and the warmth of the room were a welcome relief from the damp and chilly November night.

Seated in this richly furnished sitting room, we awaited the arrival of His Grace. He was, as everyone who had ever met him knew, a man of tremendous authority, and I felt apprehensive and somewhat overawed by the occasion. After some minutes, he entered the room and greeted us. My recollections are of a quiet-spoken, gaunt, slightly-built man, who shook hands with some reluctance. His searching eyes betrayed a calculating mentality and a degree of dominance which demanded subservience. His manner was, however, benign and welcoming.

Tea and cakes were served and the conversation centered on the pay dispute within the Garda Síochána. The Archbishop explained that he had – with a view to ending the serious unrest in the Force – been in contact with the Minister for Justice, Charles Haughey, and he had offered to persuade the men to refrain from all undisciplined action, including militant meetings, in the future. His plan was that we should leave things in his hands and that the problem would be overcome. He did not explain how it would be overcome, but requested that there be no further protest.

The primary objective of the meeting, as far as I was concerned, was the securing of a means whereby the dismissed men could be reinstated in the Force. I felt, therefore, as we took our departure at about 1:00am that the Guards should be thankful for the intervention of this highly influential figure who had taken this unusual step and who seemed sympathetic to our cause.

There were further meetings with the Archbishop in the weeks that followed. These took place at the Dublin Institute of Catholic Sociology in Eccles Street. At one such meeting, most of those involved, including the dismissed men, were gathered in a large upstairs room where it had been arranged we should meet the Archbishop. As we sat in a wide semi-circle, around a glowing coal-fire, I recall the sense of nervous apprehension that prevailed. After all, it was not every day that any of us would come face-to-face with such an important figure. Conversation portrayed the unease of those present, as we awaited the appearance of the great man through the open doorway. After what seemed an eternity, the sound of muted voices floated upwards from the hallway below. The sound of ascending footsteps, and the swish of his clerical garb as it almost dusted the well-polished floor, heralded the approach of the awesome Archbishop of Dublin.

We all rose respectfully to our feet, and remained standing until he was seated in an elaborately carved armchair in the centre of the room. His friendly, serene composure soon created a relaxed atmosphere throughout the room, and inhibitions gradually diminished. The men were not slow to voice their sense of grievance, and the Archbishop was anxious to assure them of his concern for their well-being. He commented on the hardships of police work, and how he felt sympathy for Guards on traffic duty: "I always feel sorry for those men when I drive through Donnybrook, especially in inclement weather."

In the course of a frank discussion, we explained the circumstances which had given rise to the protests and sought assurances that the dismissed men would be reinstated. The Archbishop, in turn, sought assurances that there would be no further protest meetings. We gave him the best pledge possible. Our primary concern was the reinstatement of the dismissed men. He stressed that there should be no further protests, that all would be well if matters were left in his hands, and with this he opened and spread his delicate hands and said: "Leave all this in my hands." He concluded the meeting by saying, "Your Guardian Angels will look after you all". I looked across the room into the eyes of those young men who had lost their jobs.

Archbishop McQuaid was to play a significant role in the negotiations which eventually led to the settlement of this dispute and the reinstatement of the dismissed men. I did not realize it at the time, but some thirty-seven years later Father Fehily, by then Monsignor Fehily, informed me that the then Taoiseach, Sean Lemass, and the then Justice Minister, Charles Haughey, were present in an adjoining room while we were speaking to His Grace on that memorable occasion. However, McQuaid makes no reference to their presence in his archival notes of the event.

Appendix

The Development of Labour Relations

A Historical Background

When plans for the formation of the Garda Síochána were being considered in 1922, there were in existence three forces of law and order in Ireland. These were the soon to be disbanded RIC; the Republican Police of the IRA; and the Dublin Metropolitan Police. The latter was never disbanded, but was amalgamated with the newly-founded Garda Síochána in 1925

Later, in 1939–'40 several hundred men were recruited, as a temporary measure, to form what was known as the *Taca Síochána*. Their recruitment was intended as an emergency back-up force to cope with problems emerging from the Second World War. Unlike the regular serving members of the Garda Síochána, they had no permanency of employment or entitlement to pension. It was a typical bureaucratic reaction to an unforeseen and unpredictable situation. This recruitment policy was perceived by the established members of the Force as undermining pay and conditions, and was resented by many. The position adopted by the Representative Bodies is not recorded, but it is unlikely that they would have had any influence on the decision. However, the Taca members were *de facto* full members of the Garda Síochána. They wore the same uniform and had all the powers and duties of the Garda Síochána. Indeed, as the youngest element in the Force, they were very much at the coalface for everyday duties. They were stationed almost exclusively in Dublin.

The Taca Síochána were eventually integrated into the Garda Síochána. But it was nearly 20 years later, after much wrangling and protracted negotiations with the Department of Justice, that the so-called temporary Taca service was fully recognised as Garda service for pension purposes. By which time, of course, many had died or retired, and the issue had become more or less irrelevant. Many of those who joined the Taca Síochána went on to achieve high positions in the Garda Síochána, including the rank of Commissioner.

The change in official status, brought about by the amalgamation of the DMP and the Garda Síochána in 1925, was largely a cosmetic exercise. The DMP effectively became the Dublin Metropolitan Division of the Garda Síochána. While pay, allowances, and such matters were administered under the Garda Síochána there was little change in the day-to-day life of those serving in Dublin City. Except for some minor changes, such as buttons, badges and insignia, uniforms remained the same. The police, who were now called *Gardai*, still performed the long-established system of shift work, continued to occupy the same old buildings and coped with the same old problems. The system of promotion within the Dublin Metropolitan Division (DMD) remained largely unchanged for many years. The ranks of Station Sergeant and Staff Sergeant were exclusively Metropolitan features and did not exist outside Dublin – not even in the larger cities and towns. Transfers to rural stations were exceptional and promotions were exclusively within the Division. They were greatly dependent for their powers on the Dublin Police Act.

The Garda Síochána had inherited much of the disciplinary code of the RIC and the DMP. Official attitudes on industrial relations in the Force were such that there was little encouragement for any sort of discussion on trade unionism or freedom of association. The Department of Justice exercised a great degree of authority in the administration of the Force, and anything remotely approaching trade unionism was akin to high treason.

The Representative Bodies operated in an atmosphere unsympathetic to any need for change. Consequently, little thought was ever given to the possibility of bringing about change. This is not necessarily to lay blame solely at the feet of the Representative Bodies. It is probably fair to say that the term 'industrial relations' was beyond the Pale as far as members of the Garda Síochána were concerned. That this should be so is perhaps understandable, when it is realized that the majority of the Force was on the verge of retirement and had no interest in change. Their immediate and urgent concern was for money. There was naturally less enthusiasm to rock the boat from those who had been through difficult and exacting times in the early years. Rather, their thoughts were now focused on retirement and their pensions.

A flavour of the official attitude on industrial relations, inherited by the Representative Bodies from the very beginning, may be gleaned from a document which I discovered in The National Archives many years after my retirement.

This document showed that on 25th October 1924 an article in the *'Irish Worker'* claimed that there was a great opportunity to form a policemen's union, embracing the DMP and the newly-formed Civic Guard. It offered to help in organising such a union. Nine days later the Commissioner of the DMP, General W. R. E. Murphy, submitted a report to the Minister for Justice, Kevin O'Higgins, in which he, "begged to state that the police have no idea of setting up a police union in the Dublin Metropolitan Police." He went on to state:

> "the one question causing discussion is the fear of being transferred outside the Dublin Metropolitan Police area – if amalgamation takes place." General Murphy's report claimed that discussion among the men centred on such issues as being transferred out of the DMP, Civic Guard officers being brought in over them, the present DMP Commissioner (General Murphy) remaining, being obliged to wear uniform off duty, and carry sticks – like the Civic Guards. He went on to state that the men were concerned that the methods and systems of the DMP might be changed, claiming that they joined the DMP because they liked it, and that they would not join the Guards. They were disquieted that they were now becoming Guards. In their eyes the Dublin Metropolitan Police was the most select corps and that in the event of such changes they intended to retire."

Not exactly a vote of confidence in the new Garda Síochána.

The General concluded his report as follows:

> "Amalgamation is the sole cause of any uneasiness that exists. There is nothing to contain the faintest suspicion that the

Force is not contented and happy. I have been able to remedy various repressive regulations from the past regime. The Representative Body considers that everything possible is being done to make the Force a happy one, and undoubtedly made to feel that they are treated kindly. The Representative Body is not the least afraid to ventilate grievances."

General Murphy was Deputy Commissioner of the Dublin Metropolitan Division during my early years of service. I do not recall much consideration ever having been given to the Representative Body in those years. Certainly, had he been privy to the views then being widely expressed by the man on the beat, he would have had a different view of that most happy and contented state of morale he had so eloquently proclaimed thirty years earlier. An indication of the status of the Representative Bodies, many years later, may be gleaned from the question then put to me by a very senior officer: "How did you ever become involved with that crowd?"

The Kildare mutiny

The Kildare Mutiny occurred when the assembled recruits for the Garda Síochána, who were in temporary accommodation at the RDS in Ballsbridge in early 1922, were transferred to the Military Barracks at Kildare in April of that year. But trouble had been brewing before their departure from Ballsbridge. Within weeks of their arrival at the Kildare Barracks the Guards rebelled over perceived injustices in the formation of the new Force. A rebel faction seized control of the Depot, refused to listen to Commissioner Staines, and demanded the removal of newly-appointed officers.

Whatever about the ultimate motives of some of the participants, anger at the appointment of former members of the RIC to positions of authority in the fledgling Garda Síochána lay at the heart of the trouble. The RIC was being disbanded under the 1921 Treaty and a replacement police force was urgently required. The new Force was largely recruited from the young men of the old IRA flying columns who, not unnaturally, resented the appointment to senior rank of those perceived as former enemies. It was an erroneous perception, because all of the

RIC men so appointed had rendered singular service to the nationalist, Republican, cause. Further, these men were professional policemen and their discipline, training and experience were invaluable in the onerous task of creating a police force to fill the void left by the defunct RIC. Many, including my own father, had been in the service of Michael Collins. Others had acted with great sympathy and understanding for the Republican cause during the Black and Tan period, and all had been vouched-for in the highest echelons of the Provisional Government. Indeed, Michael Collins was so incensed at this turn in events that he threatened to resign if his word on the RIC men was not accepted.

A stand-off ensued, with Commissioner Staines digging in at his Headquarters in Little Denmark Street, while the rebel faction held control in Kildare. However, coinciding with the first bombardment of the Four Courts by Free State soldiers on 28th June 1922, Staines resumed contact with the Depot in Kildare, and some two weeks later the rebel committee surrendered control of the Depot pending an inquiry into the affair.

My involvement in labour relations

It was in the Spring of 1944 that the Dublin Metropolitan class was selected from our squad of eighty recruits. Before being sent to our new stations, we were given a crash-course on our new careers as city cops. This consisted primarily of a series of lectures on laws and regulations exclusive to the Dublin Metropolitan Division. Sergeant Barney O'Connor, from Pearse Street station gave these lectures during those final weeks in the training depot. Barney, a well-seasoned sergeant who had joined the DMP over twenty years before, was a man of firm conviction. As he thumbed his dog-eared police manual, he declared with conviction: "Lads, ye can forget about all those laws you have learned. This," as he pounded his well-worn copy of the Dublin Police Act, "is the only law that counts from now on!" Such was his perception of our requirements for a career in the DMD. It became evident during the years that followed that life in the DMD had little in common with life in the rest of the Force.

By the time I had completed twelve years service and over thirty years had elapsed since the Kildare Mutiny challenge to authority, I had become increasingly aware of the many shortcomings and seemingly unnecessary frustrations of daily life in the Garda Síochána. I had on a few occasions taken senior officers at their word when, in the course of inspections, they extended the routine invitation: "Any complaints?" It was, strange as it may now seem, almost unheard of that such a call be taken at face value – even when invited to do so. I may have been naive in taking the invitation seriously, or in believing that something might be achieved by raising simple issues such as working conditions. By way of modest protest, I wished to expose this obviously pointless exercise, which was being repeated *ad nauseam* year-in-year-out without the slightest pretence at sincerity.

A consequence of my actions was that in 1956 Edward Brady, approached me with the suggestion that I should allow my name to go forward as a District Representative to the Representative Bodies. Prior to my involvement in 1956, my contact with the Representative Body was quite limited, as was the case with most members of the Force. However, I was aware that P. J. Gallagher, the first General Secretary of the Representative Bodies, had an office at Headquarters. I had met him once in his office on a personal matter in 1946 and found him to be a most friendly and approachable man who seemed only too willing to be of service whenever he could. I was then twenty-three years of age and just three years into my career. I came away with a feel-good attitude towards this kindly man as well as an appreciation of his role. I understand that Gallagher held the position of General Secretary for 22 or 23 years until his death in 1957.

Those who sought to improve the working conditions during the early decades of the Force were obliged to operate within a very restricted form of industrial relations. There little support or enthusiasm in those early years for what would have been perceived as radical thinking in a member of the Garda Síochána. Emigration was at its highest level since the Famine of 1847, and many of those at home were dependent on the remittances sent back by emigrants. Job security was non-existent for most. Hence there was great emphasis placed on the Civil Service or the Guards as a secure career for life.

In such a climate there was little scope for radical thinking – not to mention protest. If you did not like it there were many to take your place. The older Guards who then formed the majority in the Force – with families to rear and educate and with pensions in mind – were not fertile material for trade-union membership. 1950s Ireland had changed little from the times of Parnell and Davitt, and the Garda Síochána had inherited the disciplinary attitudes of the RIC. In such an atmosphere, the suggestion of an outsider advising on anything savouring of trade unionism would have been received with horror. It was completely out of the question that anybody – other than the establishment – should have any say whatsoever in the running of the Garda Síochána.

The Representative Bodies made genuine and sincere attempts to improve the lot of the Force over the years. However, making representations, either by written submissions or the occasional deputation to the Minister for Justice, was a bureaucratic and unsatisfactory process. It was not until the introduction of Conciliation and Arbitration schemes for the public service in the 1950s that there was any sign of a departure from this archaic form of representation.

Unfortunately, the Representative Bodies were unaware of the need to keep in touch with their grass-roots. Consequently interest in Representative Body affairs declined. And it was not until 1961 that the fall-out from an unpopular Conciliation Agreement brought about a more receptive and enlightened approach to new ideas. The Representative Bodies benefited from the reforms in the regulations and were enabled to develop into modern and more democratic organisations. This was particularly so in the case of the lower ranks.

The primary purpose and policy of a police force is the maintenance of law and order. Trade unions, in the interests of their members, sometimes feel obliged to use the strike weapon which often leads to police intervention. There are some who feel that the Force should have the right to strike and that the absence of full trade union status diminishes the power of their organisation – as well as infringing their natural rights to withhold their labour. In pursuit of such a policy the Garda Síochána and its predecessors the RIC and the DMP has always been precluded from going on strike.

From time to time there have been calls for a change in this regard, but I believe that this would be a mistake, as a conflict of interest would arise. However, because of this restriction, the State has an obligation to ensure that the Force is afforded the benefits which might be reasonably attained as the result of going on strike. As the Encyclical *Rerum Novarum* proclaimed on the subject of strikes, the laws should forestall and prevent such troubles from arising; they should lend their influence and authority to the removal in good time of the causes which lead to conflicts between employers and employed. The introduction of Conciliation and Arbitration schemes may be seen as a positive step in this direction. Larger employers of labour usually have special departments to deal with industrial relations problems, such as employees' contracts, promotions, discipline and general grievances. Likewise, many unions have specialists trained and assigned to deal with such matters.

The greatest hurdle to overcome is often the appointment of an arbitrator acceptable to both sides. Such arbitrators are impartial, disinterested professionals who, having listened to both parties, decide in favour of one or the other. Such decisions are not binding, but the record shows that, in the case of the Garda Síochána, Government has always honoured the findings of arbitrators. Nowadays, dealings between management and unions have been charactererized by mutual respect – however grudging in some cases. This attitude of mutual confidence has fostered better relations than formerly prevailed. However, relations between government and its employees can prove contentious when the government, as employer in the public sector, is operating an incomes policy as part of overall economic strategy.

The Dublin Committee Assignment

Little did I anticipate the course events would take when in 1956 I agreed to allow my name to go forward as a candidate in the forthcoming elections to the Garda Representative Bodies. At first, I was a District Representative on what was known as the Dublin Metropolitan Selection Committee – which I shall henceforth simply refer to as the Dublin Committee. This committee was most likely an inheritance from the days of the old DMP – as similar committees did not exist elsewhere in the Garda Síochána. The committee elected me to the Representative Body for Guards (RBG) two years later. In the years that followed my life in the Garda Síochána would become evermore bound up with industrial relations in the Force.

The Dublin Committee comprised representatives of all ranks up to and including Inspector. Meetings were held twice yearly, and only members of the committee were permitted to attend. The sole purpose of such meetings was the election of representatives to the Representative Bodies, and no meeting could be held without official permission. This latter point became a major issue some years later. However, these meetings were an opportunity to highlight grievances. Resolutions were passed on a wide variety of subjects, and these were forwarded to the Representative Bodies for consideration. Initially, I found these committee meetings something of a sham. There was little knowledge of procedures, and it was obvious that serious reforms were necessary if the deliberations were ever to mean anything. The important matter of giving the Representative Bodies more teeth was never addressed.

I should mention here that the committee had no powers whatsoever, other than being granted permission to hold one-day meetings during official working hours twice per year. No serious recognition or status was afforded this committee by the Representative Bodies, the Commissioner or senior officers. There was nothing in the Representative Bodies Regulations at that time which gave the Dublin Committee status or authority. Its role was nothing more than procedural – to send representatives on to the Representative Bodies. I eventually concluded that deliberations of the committee were meaningless and were not taken seriously. In any event the new-look committee of 1958 endeavoured to change any such perceptions by trying to make a greater impact on the Representative Bodies. A special pay claim on behalf of the DMD was compiled and submitted to the office of the Representative Bodies at Garda Headquarters, with a request that it be forwarded to the Minister for Justice. There was no response whatsoever - not even an acknowledgement - to this initiative, from either the Representative Bodies or the Deputy Commissioner of the DMD, to whom we had also sent a copy.

Another initiative by the Committee was the taking of court action to secure an electoral franchise for members of the Force. Most people nowadays would find it hard to believe that until 1960 members of the Garda Síochána were denied the franchise in either national or local elections.

No secretarial services whatsoever were available to the committee. Meetings could be held only with the explicit permission of the Commissioner. Funds could not be solicited or held, and there could be no association with any organization or group outside of the Garda Síochána. Was it any wonder, then, that a high degree of apathy prevailed for such a long time? Considering the average age-levels of the Force towards the end of the 1950s, the apathy of members, the general economic climate, and the state of industrial relations generally, it was not surprising that there was only limited support or encouragement for those who voiced the need for reform. Nevertheless, in the light of subsequent events, it is difficult to understand the lack of response to our quite reasonable requests. At the time, the heavy hand of discipline was always raised in the background, and the threat of transfer was ever present.

From 1958 onwards, the newly elected Dublin Committee adopted a policy aimed at securing a more independent role for the DMD. Efforts were made to stimulate interest in the committee throughout the Division by convening meetings in some Districts. Advice was sought from leading trade unionists - as well as the Dublin Institute of Adult Education. This institution was founded by the Archbishop of Dublin, Most Rev. John Charles McQuaid, and was active in promoting the interests of trade unions. I had discussions with the officers of the Irish Congress of Trade Unions[*] and they intimated that they were willing to become involved in seeking trade-union status for the Representative Bodies. It was later put to me that had my superior officers been aware of these discussions the question of my dismissal from the Force would have arisen. Anything remotely approaching trade unionism was considered quite inappropriate for a member of the Garda Síochána.

---

[*] John Conroy, Fintan Kennedy, and Donal Nevin

There seemed little support for any ideas I had at the time about seeking support from the Irish Congress of Trade Unions. However, the Dublin Institute of Catholic Sociology was a source of encouragement in our efforts to gain some experience in the field of industrial relations. My association with the Institute had been established through my friends, Jerry Desmond and Joe Driscoll of the Technical Bureau, who introduced me to the Director, Father Thomas Fehilly. In the absence of any official support for reform of the Representative Bodies, I was very appreciative of any advice and encouragement from the Institute. Subsequently, the Institute was to play an important role in the crisis that arose in 1961, namely the Macushla Affair, and it was fortunate that good relationships had already been established before that crucial occurrence.

A member of the Representative Body

When I first arrived on the Representative Body scene in 1958, I felt that we were regarded as something of an aberration. It was a bit like Éamon de Valera's response to Ireland's position in the Commonwealth: we are in it but not of it. At least this was the perceived view of many in the DMD during those years. There was a sharp contrast in the conditions of service between Dublin and elsewhere. I had been twelve years in the Force and would have been regarded as belonging to the younger element. There were, of course, many members junior to me, but the vast majority were my seniors. The bulk of the Force, recruited in the 1920s, had not yet reached retirement age. Decisions affecting pay taken at Conciliation Council meetings were influenced by concern for the pensions of older members nearing the compulsory retirement age. The conditions of service for junior members were not perceived as of immediate concern. These could be left for another day. That day would come sooner than many expected.

Those seeking reform of the Representative Body Regulations shared a strong sense of frustration. When a new committee was elected in 1958, it was something of a triumph for the younger members: Seán O'Colmain and I were elected Chairman and Secretary respectively. Edward McNiff, an old timer, and I became representatives on the Representative Body for Guards. We were part of what might be described as a team representing the NCOs and Guards of the DMD.

The archaic regulation which required all unmarried guards, who were compelled to live in the Garda station, to return to their stations not later than 11.00 pm, even though off duty, was a particular irritant. It applied to all ages. A regulation that obliged mature men to leave a social occasion and return to barracks before 11:00pm – unless special permission was sought and granted – now seems unbelievable.

Although the Force had been established for over thirty years, living conditions in stations were quite primitive. Few stations were purpose-built and most were converted private dwellings inherited from the days of the DMP. The poor condition of these buildings was a frequent source of complaint. Personal comforts were not high on the list of priorities. Furnishings were very basic and more in keeping with standards prevalent in the 19th Century. My first issue of bed-sheets sported laundry labels dated 1912. The mess room had bare wooden dining tables typical of those in army use since the days of the First World War. Our dining room suite comprised only plain wooden benches and an ancient heavy table. There were no dining chairs, armchairs, radios or clocks. There were few pictures and there were no curtains – only wooden shutters. Recreational facilities were non-existent. Such 'luxuries' as dartboards, billiard tables and radios were later provided through self-supporting recreation committees organized by the members themselves. Even toilet paper was denied us, and it was not until the arrival of Commissioner Costigan in 1952 that we saw the beginnings of long overdue reforms in such areas. The Garda Síochána was at last to receive its quota of toilet paper!

If I was surprised and somewhat disillusioned by the difficulties experienced by the Dublin committee, I was in for an even greater surprise when I arrived at Garda Headquarters to partake in the deliberations of the Representative Bodies.

Before Time Steals the Past

Although the winds of change were ruffling industrial relations in the Ireland of the 1950s, the Garda Síochána remained locked in a virtual time warp. The disciplinary attitudes, inherited from the days of the RIC and the environment of the times, precluded any perception of the need for change. The restrictions imposed on the Representative Bodies had stifled any serious thought of reforming the regulations under which they operated. The murmurings of dissent in the 1950s went unheeded; frustration and discontent developed throughout the lower ranks. As the outmoded system of representation failed to take on board the concerns of the more progressive elements within the Force, it was inevitable that a crisis would develop. The storm broke in 1961, when an agreement on pay and allowances so disadvantaged younger members of the Force that the weaknesses in the structure of the Representative Bodies were exposed. Following public protest by members of Garda rank, a crisis situation arose as a result of the dramatic dismissal of a number of young Gardaí.

Those who had been in control of affairs for so long, namely the Department of Justice and the Garda Commissioner, sought to put a brave face on the crisis, and attempted to explain away as 'unjustified or unreasonable' the nature of the protests being made by the lower ranks. The Representative Bodies were now the *bête noire* of all those in authority. Furthermore no statement was ever issued by the Chairman or other officer of the Representative Bodies, who were in a no-win situation. To be fair, it should be said that there was at the time no precedent or provision for such a course of action. Unlike today, members of the Garda Síochána never went public on Garda matters. They were forbidden to do so. Everything was in the hands of the Commissioner, and the then incumbent, Daniel Costigan, was confronted with a situation which had not arisen since the days of the Garda Mutiny at Kildare in 1922.

During those early years, P. J. Gallagher played a major part in establishing the Representative Bodies and other welfare societies in the Garda. Chief Superintendent Tom Collins was another prominent personality who exercised a strong influence for many years. He was Chairman of the Officers' Body, and as such took the chair at all meetings of the Joint Bodies. In 1958, Inspector Harry Nangle and Sgt. Dan Fingelton, both of Headquarters, took control of the NCOs Body as Chairman and Secretary respectively. These were all men of the first generation of Guards, and were at the time of my arrival approaching their final years of service. Seán O'Colmáin, a forceful and energetic personality from the Dublin Committee, was, like myself, a representative of a later generation.

Subsequently, representatives of the younger members of the Force came on the scene, and they were to play an important and decisive role in shaping the course of events. These were the young Guards of the Macushla Affair of 1961 – which will be examined later. The most prominent of these, as far as I can recall, were Jack Marrinan, Frank Mullen, Mick Harlow, Donal Murphy and Dick Keating, some of whom were to be dismissed from the Force but later reinstated. There were many others, who played a significant role during the early years of the organisation, but strictures of time and space require that I forego reference to any but those most pertinent to my story.

Perhaps I will be forgiven if my thoughts linger briefly on some of those dedicated men who must remain anonymous. They are, in my view, the unsung heroes. They are mostly men whose only motivation was to see justice done and who spoke up when it was not easy or wise to do so. Often in the face of bureaucratic and inefficient authority, such men risked censure or worse by bringing the most glaring injustices or petty frustrations to notice. Indeed, it was not unknown for their attempts at reform to attract derision from those most likely to benefit from a successful outcome of their efforts. They would be reminded that having aspirations for change was not necessarily the best road to a successful career. Attendance at unofficial meetings, standing at collection tables seeking funds, circulating notices, and endeavouring to articulate the problems of others quite often attracted a degree of undeserved censure. The terms 'crank', or 'header' were often applied to those who sought nothing more than simple fair play for all. I believe that, even if some were not motivated by the highest ideals, they were mostly sincere and genuine individuals who were unfortunately vocal before their time.

The Last Straw

For over thirty years, P. J. Gallagher had carried out the duties of full-time General Secretary. There was, however, no statutory provision for such a position. Following Gallagher's death, Sergeant Dan Fingelton was elected to succeed him, at a meeting of the Joint Representative Bodies in 1958. For reasons best known to himself, Fingelton chose to remain at his Weights & Measures desk in the depot and regarded his new position as part-time. I was greatly surprised at this decision, which was accepted without demur by the newly-elected representatives.

Control of the Representative Bodies had always been in the hands of the establishment. All arrangements for the election of representatives were determined by 'B' Branch, and Divisional and District Officers. The rank-and-file members of the Force had no say in the convening of elections. The management of Representative Body affairs devolved largely on personnel at Headquarters and a few interested officers. It also has to be said that there was very little interest throughout the Force in the election or appointment of representatives. Some of the younger members rightly perceived this widespread apathy as a major handicap. Those of us who had taken control in the Dublin Committee were determined to redress the issue as a matter of priority.

The regulations provided for a separate Representative Body for each of the different ranks, but *de facto* there really was no 'Representative Body for Guards'. Major issues were considered only at meetings held jointly with the Representative Bodies of the Officers and the NCOs. Day-to-day administration was from an office at Garda Headquarters in John's Road. About nine members of the Force, none of them members of the Representative Bodies, staffed it full-time. In the light of subsequent events, it is difficult to understand such a situation – representatives of the majority Garda rank had no direct full-time management of their own organisation.

There was a proposal by members of the Guard's Body that, as secretary of this Body, I should be employed full-time in this office. The proposal was fudged and brushed aside at a meeting of the Joint Representative Bodies, which was largely in the hands of the Officers' Body. I was left to conduct the business of the Representative Body for Guards in my spare time from my home in Dún Laoghaire. The practice of addressing all official correspondence to the Joint Representative Bodies at John's Road had developed over the years. Consequently those holding positions on the nominally separate Bodies were totally sidelined in the day-to-day running of affairs. Being Secretary of the Representative Body for Guards was a sick joke. The same, of course, was true of other positions, such as Chairman, of either of the two junior Bodies.

The position of Secretary of the NCOs' Body was somewhat different. Fingelton held that position, but then he also had the non-statutory position of General Secretary of the Joint Representative Bodies. This latter position had evolved over the years since the formation of the Representative Bodies. It was a situation which seemed acceptable, or at least survived without question, until the first murmuring protests were voiced towards the end of the 1950s when a younger generation, with somewhat different ideas on the running of their organisation sought to assert an increasing influence on the affairs of the Representative Bodies.

Human nature being what it is, the older, and more entrenched personnel resented change. Indeed, tradition and discipline ordained that senior ranks should always run the show; the lower ranks were to be seen but not heard. For the present, their quest for influence was to be resisted. What had come about was that the Guards' Body had been subsumed – along with the other two Bodies – into one organisation, namely The Joint Representative Bodies. The Chairman of the Joint Representative Bodies was always the Chief Superintendent from the Officers' Body, and as events turned out, this proved very unsatisfactory for the junior ranks.

Such developments were, in my view, a most retrograde step. It was bad enough that the Representative Bodies had little status and very limited powers of representation. That the office of full-time General Secretary - which had functioned with official approval over the years - should now be arbitrarily set aside by the new incumbent, seemed incredible. It is difficult to explain the motivation for such a decision. In the light of subsequent developments it is difficult to understand how the largest numerical group (Guards) acquiesced to such an arrangement. No doubt, early experiences in the Garda Síochána and the stringent economic conditions of the times were major influences in shaping the attitudes of men approaching retirement.

The mid 1950s witnessed the replacement of the founding generation by younger men. The first winds of change were blowing. As the decade drew to a close, younger members of the Force were becoming aware of the need for substantial improvement in their access to channels of representation. It became clear to a few of us that moulds had to be broken. Efforts were made to influence and change the power structure, as well as the *modus operandi* of the Representative Bodies. The Dublin Committee had submitted its own pay claim. Commissioner Costigan was aware of the enthusiasm of this committee, but unfortunately failed to intervene or give support. In his book on the Garda Síochána,[*] the late Gregory Allen gives a detailed account of the difficulties created for Commissioner Costigan by the obfuscation rampant in the so-called Joint Representative Bodies – despite the efforts of the junior ranks to simplify matters.

In the run-up to the elections of 1959, some days before Christmas, the late Bob Greene and I, on behalf of the Dublin Committee, circulated from Dún Laoghaire Station to every Garda station in Ireland about two thousand copies of a printed leaflet advocating the need for a keener interest in the forthcoming elections. Cost of postage was borne by the committee. The objective was to stimulate interest in the affairs of the Representative Body and ensure a more democratic and representative election, which would return new faces with new ideas. I believe that this did indeed have the effect of changing at least some of the personnel on the junior Bodies. However, the pace of events was to overtake such tentative steps.

As 1961 drew to a close, the winds of change of the late 1950s were fanned to a storm by reactions to the pay agreements in 1961. It was a storm that was to change dramatically the set-up of future joint representation within the Garda Síochána. What became known as The

---

[*] Gregory Allen, *The Garda Síochána: Policing Independent Ireland 1922-82* Gill & Macmillan.

Macushla Affair led to new structures and, more importantly, to new attitudes both within and towards the Representative Bodies - in particular towards the Representative Body for Guards.

When young Garda Pat Lally, the most junior member of the new Representative Body for Guards, took the chairman's seat at the first joint meeting of the three Representative Bodies, held under the new 1962 Regulations, the mould was finally broken. Joint meetings of the three Representative Bodies would henceforth have a more equitable and meaningful purpose. The struggle for real recognition had just begun. It would be another year before the first fruits fell from the branches. I was pleased to have played a part in the chain of events, which from that day onwards saw the Representative Body for Guards take its rightful place in the cause of Garda welfare. Things would never be the same again.

Feet of Clay

Over the years the three Representative Bodies had coalesced and to all intents and purposes functioned as one organisation. The regulations provided nothing more than that the three bodies might agree to meet as a Joint Representative Body (JRB). The office of the Representative Body at John's Road served the needs of the voluntary Garda Societies, such as the Medical Aid and Benevolent Societies, as well as those of the General Secretary of this joint Body. The death of P. J. Gallagher had left a void. He had functioned as a successful and unchallenged General Secretary since the foundation of the Force. I have never discovered any provision in statutory legislation (Representative Body Regulations), which authorized the provision of a full-time General Secretary, or the employment of a full-time staff who were all members of the Force. The criterion for their employment was not clear, and their appointment to the office never came before the Representative Bodies during my years as a representative. Indeed, we were never quite sure who was employed there.

The individual Representative Bodies were not in a position to make separate direct use of the office. It could be said that, *de facto*, there really were no separate Bodies. Certainly, the RBG never functioned as an independent Body. The facility of having such an office was at the behest and within the gift of the Commissioner or the Department of Justice. Commissioner Costigan, when defending the official line at the time of the Macushla Affair in 1961, forcibly made the point that the office facilities, with a full-time staff, were being provided at the expense of the State. To the best of my recollection, he made much play of the fact there were up to nine members of the Force employed there. The RBG certainly had little or no access to such a workforce. The Commissioner's remarks were typical of the reaction of the Establishment, which was endeavouring to dig itself out of hole, namely the crisis brought about by the failure to advance industrial relations over the years. The official response to the crisis was both ham-fisted and ineffectual.

At the time of my arrival on the scene in 1958, it was obvious that the two Bodies representing the lower ranks had become subservient to the Officers' Body. Matters of a substantive nature such as pay, allowances and conditions of service were discussed and decided upon only at meetings of the JRB. Such meetings were convened only when the Officers' Body so decided. While it may serve little purpose to dwell at any great length on the details of meetings of the Representative Bodies during those years, I cannot resist recalling some experiences and impressions gained at that time.

All meetings took place in the Library at the Depot, twice yearly – in late spring or early summer, and shortly before Christmas. The duration of each session was usually ten to fourteen days. Travel expenses and subsistence allowances were paid, such attendance being regarded as an occasion of duty. I can well recall my inner personal reactions to the manner in which the business of those meetings was conducted. At first I did not know what to expect. I assumed that meetings would be conducted in a businesslike manner and with a high degree of commitment. It soon became clear that these meetings were convened without any prior consultation with the junior Bodies. This might occur at any time, with little notice being sent to the participants. Two or three such meetings took place over the entire session. There was no advance consultation with members on the compilation of an agenda. As soon as members of the Officers' Body entered the library there was a marked change in the atmosphere. An air of authority prevailed. Why not? Were we not still on duty? We almost stood to attention until the chairman took his seat.

This was in marked contrast to the casual disposition of representatives when meetings of the two junior Bodies were convened separately. The efforts which some of us made to instil enthusiasm into such meetings all too often fell on stony ground. For instance, punctuality was not a strong point with some members, and as there was no agenda circulated in advance time hung heavily on their hands. Hours were given over to card-playing and shopping. I soon concluded that these meetings, intended for serious discussions on the welfare of the Force, were taken less seriously than I would have wished. My youthful idealism was taking a knock. I had come to the high altar to contribute rather than to worship, and found the gods had feet of clay.

Matters of major importance were discussed only at joint meetings of all three Bodies. Such meetings, it seemed, were convened at the behest of the Officers' Body. The NCOs' and Guards' Bodies were left to their own devices for most of these twice-yearly sessions. In regard to anything other than pay, allowances, and pensions, I have no recollection of the Officers' Body having ever sat down with the NCOs' and Guards' Bodies to discuss their particular problems. There was no attempt to organise constructive all-embracing discussion of the many problems affecting the daily lives of the rank and file. Was it any wonder that coming events would cast their shadows and shatter the status quo?

The junior Bodies held joint *ad hoc* meetings, discussing matters apparently of no concern or interest to the Officer's Body. The outcome of these discussions was usually very obscure. As there was seldom, if ever, a pre-arranged agenda, it was a matter of taking on board whatever seemed the most urgent or important issue of the day. The Secretary, who had chosen to act only in a part-time capacity, would write up an account of these deliberations and pass it on to the office of the Representative Body at John's Road, from where representations would eventually be made to the Commissioner. No doubt, he was simply following procedures which had evolved over many years. There was no follow-up information on the representations, and by the time of the next session – in about six month's time – it was difficult to say what progress, if any, had been made. From time to time, a circular would arrive from Headquarters giving the response to some of the representations made. Such circulars were infrequent and certainly never dwelt on the need to support or reform the Representative Bodies.

It was an archaic and unsatisfactory means of conducting industrial relations. The Garda Review, the only organ of the Representative Bodies, expressed a limited degree of independence, but it seldom reflected the specific concerns of the Representative Bodies. It was clear that reforms were needed.

Sit Down, Guard!

Prior to the granting of a Conciliation and Arbitration Scheme to the Garda Síochána, the Representative Bodies were in a pretty weak position. Representations were made from time to time, and the decisions of the Minister for Justice or the Commissioner simply had to be accepted, as there were no means of appeal or redress.

When Conciliation and Arbitration Schemes were first granted to the public service - during the 1950s - the Representative Bodies sought similar treatment for the Garda Síochána. At first there was resistance to the proposal from the Department of Justice, but the Government agreed in 1958 to a Conciliation and Arbitration Scheme for ranks up to and including Inspectors

I had just been elected by the Dublin Committee as a delegate to the Representative Body for Guards (RBG), and I recall my earliest experience of the so-called Joint Representative Bodies. A joint meeting of the three Representative Bodies had been convened to consider the draft of a Conciliation and Arbitration Scheme. From a seat at the head of large table, and flanked on either side by Supt. D. Corcoran of Headquarters (Secretary of the Officers' Body) and Sergeant D. Fingelton (General Secretary), Chief Superintendent T. Collins, chairman of the Officers' Representative Body presided. It was assumed that the chief superintendent would automatically take the chair and there was no question of anybody else being proposed as chairman.

There was no written agenda or adoption of standing orders., The meeting commenced with the Chairman giving a brief outline of the proposed Conciliation and Arbitration Scheme and laying great stress on the Officers being excluded from the scheme. This was immediately followed by a proposal from the Officers' Body calling on the meeting to reject the scheme – on the grounds that it divided the Force by excluding the Officers.

As their newly elected secretary, I felt obliged to point out that the RBG had not received copies of the Scheme and was therefore not yet in a position to give the scheme proper consideration. I proposed that the meeting should adjourn in order to give the RBG an opportunity to meet separately and consider the scheme fully. I emphasized that the issue was of very great importance to the RBG and it should be given an opportunity to make its own decision. There was a full attendance at that meeting, but not one Guard or NCO rose to second my proposal.

As the Chairman was about to proceed, I persisted in making my point. Nothing would be lost by allowing more time for the consideration of this very important matter, I argued. However, the solitary pleadings of a junior Garda echoed hollow in such a muted assembly. My continued protests that the Garda rank was not being allowed a say in its own affairs were met with a stern rebuke from the Chairman. Loud and clear came his very firm admonition, "Sit down, Guard!" Although I continued to protest at this arbitrary and undemocratic decision, the Chairman declared that the Conciliation and Arbitration Scheme, which the Bodies had been seeking for some years, had now been rejected.

Rejection of the Scheme resulted in a very strained atmosphere between the Representative Bodies and the Department of Justice. As I recall the circumstances of the time, copies of the scheme were never circulated to individual members of the Bodies – not to mention the entire Force. As a consequence of this rejection, the Force was denied for over a year the long-sought Conciliation and Arbitration Scheme. Another year would pass before the issue was re-opened, and in the interim the important matter of pay was left in abeyance. It was my first real insight into the manner in which the affairs of the Representative Bodies were conducted, and I quickly came to realize that the RBG had a very subordinate role indeed.

The greater part of the Force was being deprived of whatever benefits might hopefully derive from this new exercise in industrial relations, without being given even an opportunity to express any opinions on the matter. The Department of Justice took great exception to the terminology used in the letter of rejection, such as, "… driving a wedge in the Force." I presume the letter was drafted by Chief Superintendent Collins and those then in charge of affairs. Certainly, the RBG had no say in the drafting of this letter.

We eventually heard further from the Chairman at a meeting of the Joint Bodies in 1959. This was to the effect that, while walking through Dublin a short time previously he had – entirely by accident it seems – bumped into Mr. Oscar Traynor, the then Minister for Justice. The Chairman claimed that he and the Minister had discussed the impasse and that the problem had been solved. He did not explain how. As a result of this very fortunate chance meeting, officers would henceforth be included in the Conciliation and Arbitration Scheme. Being on the periphery of the day-to-day operations of the Representative Bodies at the time, I cannot explain further how this resolution of the affair came about. Certainly, a chance meeting in O'Connell Street seemed a somewhat fortunate, if unlikely, coincidence. Suffice it to say that the Conciliation and Arbitration Scheme came into operation for all ranks in 1959. That's the way things were done.

A consolidated pay claim for all ranks was later compiled at the Representative Body's office in John's Road. This was largely the work of Dick Rice, a clerk, who seemed to take over as General Secretary following the death of Sergeant P.J. Gallagher in 1957, and the decision of Sergeant Fingleton not to become a full-time secretary. In any event, at a meeting of the JRB in 1958, it was proposed (not by any member of the RBG) that Dick Rice be recommended for special promotion, as a replacement for Gallagher. The Commissioner accepted the recommendation.

Garda Edward McEniff, my colleague from the DMD, proposed that

I, as secretary of the Representative Body for Guards, should be assigned full-time to the office at John's Road. This proposal was fudged by Supt. Corcoran - who was attached to "B" Branch - undertaking to 'see to it'. Nothing came of the proposal and I was obliged to continue in my so-called role of secretary while still on normal outdoor duties at Dún Laoghaire. The absurdity of an elected secretary of a statutory representative organisation for the entire Garda rank having to continue on full-time regular duty was bizarre.

Charitable Donations.

In hindsight, I look back upon the appointment of our representatives under the Conciliation and Arbitration Scheme with some cynicism. The scheme, in line with similar schemes in the public service, was seen as a breakthrough in industrial relations. For the first time, representatives of the Force could participate in face-to-face discussions with the Departments of Justice and Finance on matters of pay and allowances. There was also, for the first time, provision for an independent arbitrator who would be the chairman of an Arbitration Board. Contrary to what might have been expected, the General Secretary did not take an active part in the Scheme, and I felt that this was a further downgrading of the responsibilities of his office - as he had treated his position as part-time from the very beginning.

The Officers proposed the nomination of Chief Superintendent Collins and Superintendent Corcoran as the two Garda members of the Arbitration Board. There was a decided lack of enthusiasm for the proposal, as it was considered that the officers were having too much of a say in the new Conciliation & Arbitration scheme. In a rare display of independence, Edward McEniff, my fellow Garda representative from Dublin, suggested that I should be nominated for one of the two positions. Unexpected support for this proposal came from some of the NCOs. However, in the end it was agreed that Garda Malachy Egan from Cork and Chief Superintendent Collins should represent the Force on the Arbitration Board. Egan was an old-timer who had represented the Munster area on the RBG for many years. As a senior Garda he was well known and on familiar terms with the Chairman and the older members. His nomination to the Arbitration Board was an acceptable compromise, as I was a very junior member and a newcomer on the scene. I was elected to the 'Garda Side' of the Conciliation Council and, although denied a full-time position in the office at John's Road, I quickly gained an insight into what was intended by 'representing the Force'. The ability of Guards to represent Guards and their entitlement to a separate Representative Body was considered very questionable in some quarters. I am reminded of that amusing directive in the regulations: "A sergeant or an intelligent Guard should be sent to the scene."

We had no input into the drafting of submissions to the Conciliation Council. All this was done at John's Road, and the claims were then submitted directly to the Conciliation Council without any referral to the Representative Bodies. Being prohibited from accessing professional expertise disadvantaged the 'Garda Side,' as its members had little knowledge of modern industrial relations. The first meeting of the Conciliation Council was held in the offices of the Commissioners for Charitable Donations at Upper Baggot St. In view of the total failure to achieve anything worthwhile at this meeting, I think the choice of venue added a humorous dimension to the scene. I was soon to realise that not everyone was quite as serious-minded as I had believed. In the course of the meeting I received something of a shock when I became aware that a very senior member of the 'Official Side', sitting opposite me, was fast asleep during our deliberations. The Secretary of the Department of Justice, Mr. Coyne, chaired the meeting. I was slowly being educated in the ways of officialdom. There was no agreement, and the claim went to arbitration in 1960.

In 1961, a pay claim was submitted to the Conciliation Council. The agreement reached on this claim caused considerable controversy and anger among many junior Gardaí, because those with less than four years service were excluded. As did the imposition of a deduction of £1 per week in lieu of official accommodation – so that rent allowance could be made pensionable – a concession long sought by the Representative Bodies. The good intent of this agreement was largely misunderstood and generated much unrest.

These, then, are some of my recollections of the early years of the

Conciliation and Arbitration Scheme. The following two years would witness a considerable breakthrough in the field of representation for the Garda Síochána. The RBG, elected under the 1962 Regulations, was now in a position to act independently – and did so. The new regulations permitted the Representative Bodies to solicit financial support from their members, the right to employ professional advisors and make provision for the appointment of a full-time Secretary. These were very important major concessions, which a few of us had been frustratingly advocating for some years. Their inclusion in the revised regulations was a milestone which brought the RBG in from the cold, as it were. It was now a far cry from the unquestioning acceptance which had been so much a feature of the old days. By the autumn of 1963, the RBG, acting entirely on its own initiative, had succeeded in winning a major pay claim. It had set a headline for the other two bodies and was now the dominant representative organisation. There would be no more calls of 'Sit down Guard!'

It is perhaps worth pointing out that in those years the Representative Bodies were not allowed to raise funds in support of any claims which might be considered under the Conciliation and Arbitration Scheme. The 'Establishment' was very protective of its role as Big Brother and there was a decided reluctance to afford liberties to mere public servants. Trade unionism was not permitted, and Conciliation and Arbitration Schemes were seen as an acceptable compromise on issues such as pay and allowances. Members of the Force who had little experience or knowledge of the finer points of negotiating industrial relations were at a distinct disadvantage when it came to the professional presentation of claims. In the context of the times, the Conciliation & Arbitration Scheme was an advance for the Garda Síochána. Shortcomings remained, but - as will be seen later - a combination of exceptional events radically altered the nature and course of the Representative Bodies, as well as the proceedings under the Conciliation and Arbitration Scheme.

The Macushla – No Ballroom of Romance

The Macushla Ballroom on Amiens Street was a drab four-story building in the heart of Dublin, not far from Store Street Garda Station.

It was destined to become part of the folk memory of the Garda Síochána when, in November 1961, it became the venue for a 'rebellion' by younger elements in the Force. When news broke of the pay claim awarded in 1961, there was an instantly hostile reaction. This came mostly from junior members, some of whom had received nothing. Secretive meetings took place, principally in the Dublin area. This led in turn to a large public meeting in the Machushla Ballroom.

As a member of the Conciliation Council that had agreed the pay claim, I did not, of course, have the confidence of those who organized those meetings. The people involved were all young Gardaí who obviously had no confidence in their Representative Body, and which they perceived as having failed them. The fact that the RBG had been moribund was not at all obvious to them. There was absolutely no reaction from those who had day-to-day control of Representative Body affairs, or from any of the elected members of the three Bodies. A policy of keeping a low profile was adopted by those who should have been to the forefront in responding to developments. I was very concerned at the turn of events.

The meeting arranged for the Machushla Ballroom on 4th November 1961 was widely publicized. Public meetings by members of the Force were strictly forbidden at the time, but the mood was such that the younger members were quite rebellious and were determined to ignore the regulations. As a representative of Garda rank, I felt somehow responsible for the situation which had developed, notwithstanding the difficulties I was experiencing within the organisation. My fellow District Representative, Garda Paul Hedderman, discussed the situation with me and agreed that, if possible, we should attend the Macushla meeting. From my home in Sandycove on the morning of the meeting, I took the unorthodox step of phoning Assistant Commissioner William Quinn, then in charge of the Dublin Metropolitan Area, to the effect that I was anxious to attend the proposed illegal meeting and requested his authorization. He refused to give such authorization.

Paul Hedderman and I drove to the vicinity of the Macushla Ballroom in time for the meeting and debated at length whether or not we should attend. In the end we decided not to do so, as support or encouragement for our intercession was not forthcoming from any quarter. We reluctantly abandoned our attempt to play a helpful role. Perhaps on this occasion the Commissioner, Mr. Costigan, or his Deputies, should have taken their best walking canes in hand, gone to the meeting, addressed the men, and given an undertaking to look into the whole matter of representation. But any such suggestion seemed a bridge too far. For me it demonstrated the lack of leadership that prevailed in the Garda Síochána.

Commissioner Costigan issued a statement at the time. One of the points he made was that nine members of the Force were employed permanently and full-time at the office of the Representative Body Office in John's Road. He was technically correct in saying so. However, he failed to touch on the reality that the Representative Body of the rank and file had no input into such staffing and that its Secretary was in no position to properly discharge the duties of his office.

There were secret investigations by the authorities to identify those behind the Macushla Affair. Some Inspectors and Sergeants were more willing than others to comply with instructions in this regard. The entire affair caused a lot of bad feeling; deep suspicion and mistrust were generated as well as the fear of betrayal. While it would have been simple enough to do as others were doing - namely nothing - I felt obliged, as a representative of the Garda rank, to carry some responsibility for those aggrieved. I believed that they were now likely to suffer even further as a consequence of their decision to hold such protest meetings.

At that particular time, while we were on night duty at Dún Laoghaire, the Macushla meetings and the serious unrest were a constant topic of conversation. A young Garda, Frank Mullen, was my companion on patrol-car duty, and I was aware that he and a few of the younger men were involved. As the nights passed and the stress and apprehension mounted for all concerned, it was becoming clear that a proposed second Macushla meeting was not going to receive the required support. The threats of severe disciplinary measures and the absence of support from any significant source were fast becoming a matter of concern. I formed the opinion that the omens for a successful, well-attended meeting were not good. It was becoming increasingly clear that the pressure being exercised by the authorities was beginning to take effect. A few of the organisers were becoming nervous at the thought of possible dismissal. I endeavoured to give advice, which might somehow protect them from the worst effects of severe disciplinary action, and suggested that it might be to their advantage if a postponement of the proposed second meeting could be arranged.

I was not privy to the secret decisions of those at the heart of the protest. Many years later, Frank Mullen and I mused over the events of those days. We endeavoured to recall what had transpired, both prior to and immediately following the protest meetings. What follows is the gist of those recollections:

The terms of the 1961 Pay Order led to a sense of victimisation among the younger members of the Force. A small group of young men from Pearse Street Garda Station met in nearby O'Reilly's Pub and decided to hold a protest meeting at the Macushla Ballroom on 7th November. This event was publicised in the *Irish Times*. To the great surprise of the organisers, about five or six hundred Gardaí turned up. Because the holding of this meeting - contrary to disciplinary regulations - was well known to the authorities, a large force of Inspectors from the Division was in attendance outside the ballroom. They had been instructed to take the names of all those entering the ballroom. Instructions from the Commissioner had been issued and read out to all Gardaí on the previous day. The instructions were to the effect that anyone attending this meeting would, if identified, be disciplined and more serious unspecified steps would be taken against the organisers. A clear attempt was being made to intimidate the organisers in the hope of having the meeting called off. A committee of about ten was formed. Most, if not all, were young men who had served not more than two or three years, who were unmarried and were quite prepared to put their careers on the line if necessary. Although inexperienced in such matters and feeling nervous and unsure of the possible outcome, the organisers were very pleased at the support received. A Committee was formed from those who volunteered from the floor. A series of meetings in Limerick, Cork and elsewhere was planned, with a follow-up meeting in Dublin about eight days later. The affair received wide publicity in the following day's newspapers.

In the aftermath of the meeting, on the direction of Assistant Commissioner Quinn, there was a widespread inquisition by senior officers in an effort to identify as many as possible of those in sympathy with what had taken place. Officers were sent to Limerick and Cork in the hope of naming the ringleaders. Members of the committee were aware of being trailed and watched, and an air of apprehension permeated their numbers. There were rumours that sackings would follow. On the Thursday evening, news came in that eleven of the leaders, all from the Dublin area, had been dismissed. However, a 'go-slow' was instigated which caused widespread traffic chaos on the Friday evening. This received substantial press coverage, and was attributed to those in support of the dismissed men. As tension mounted, members of the Committee sought, and expected, mass written resignations by way of support. They were to be sadly disappointed. In the Dún Laoghaire area there were only three. Everyone was backing off following the dismissals and the continuing heavy-handedness of authority. Those who were deeply involved realised that they were on a downward slope, and the reality that they might soon stand alone began to dawn on them. Some were resigned to the fact that they would soon be no longer members of the Garda Síochána and without a job.

By a strange coincidence, or divine intervention, a tragic event occurred which dramatically influenced the course of events. At about 11:00 pm on the Saturday night prior to the proposed second meeting in the Macushla, Frank Mullen and I, while on patrol-car duty, were directed to the scene of a fatal traffic accident at Stradbrook Road, Blackrock. To our shock and surprise the victim was the wife of Assistant Commissioner Quinn. Later, in the early hours of that morning at the Dún Laoghaire mess-room, this tragic event and the difficulties surrounding recent happenings were the subject of intense discussion. I suggested to Frank that - all things considered - it would be an ideal moment to show sympathy and support for the Assistant Commissioner. In the event, an expression of sympathy was made public and the proposed second meeting at the Macushla was cancelled. A window of opportunity had been opened.

Burning the Midnight Oil

Frank Mullen and I had long discussions during the remainder of that night. As was our custom, we went to 5:00 am Mass in Donnybrook. On our return journey, a Garda stopped us in Blackrock. He informed us that a message had been received to the effect that the second meeting in the Macushla, that day, Sunday, had been cancelled. Apparently, somebody in Kevin Street station had sent out such a message on the teleprinter. We never established who was responsible, but agreed that it would be best to confirm beyond doubt that the meeting had been cancelled. Later that morning we arranged for a local art student to print a large banner bearing the words:

Meeting Cancelled Due to Recent Tragic Event

and this was draped across the main entrance to the Macushla Ballroom.

By evening time the news bulletins featuring the 'Garda protest' had a conciliatory ring, reflecting the sense of responsibility shown by the protesters in their response to the tragic death of the wife of their Assistant Commissioner. This, they stated, was a gesture which should be appreciated. Wheels were turning within wheels!

Towards the end of the week, my own involvement with the Dublin Institute of Catholic Sociology was about to draw me further into the Macushla Affair. Archbishop McQuaid had become concerned at the deteriorating situation, and Father Fehily - Director of the Institute - contacted me and others with a view to arranging a meeting with Archbishop McQuaid.

In the diocesan archives I find reference by the Archbishop to only one such meeting, although there were undoubtedly two or three. From Dr. McQuaid's records it now emerges that he, on his own initiative, had requested the Minister for Justice, Mr.Haughey, to come to see him. When Mr. Haughey arrived in Killiney, at 5:00 pm on Sunday, November 12, the Archbishop told the Minister that the matter was being handled badly, with the dismissal of eleven young men. He suggested that something must be seriously wrong when decent members of the Force felt obliged to act in such unorthodox ways, and urged Mr. Haughey to bring an end to the matter.

The Archbishop offered to persuade the men to guarantee that there would be no more meetings, and Mr.Haughey expressed his satisfaction with that. However, he was reluctant at first to reinstate the eleven dismissed men. Eventually, he agreed that discipline, which was his main worry, could best be restored by the goodwill that such a reinstatement would generate. There had been a shooting on the border that day, and the Archbishop felt that it was imperative to resolve the Garda problem. He told Minister Haughey that he would ask Father Fehily to bring some Garda representatives to him that night and stressed how necessary it was that Mr. Haughey, as a new Minister, should not make any mistake in his early days in office. Moreover, he said he was sure he could guarantee the goodwill of the Guards. Mr. Haughey elaborated on all he had done for Garda welfare and now promised that he would re-examine their grievances in the area of representation at grassroots level.

Late that same night, Frank Mullen, Seán O'Colmáin and I met with the Archbishop at his residence in Killiney. Father Fehily, who drove us to Killiney from his office in Eccles Street, arranged this meeting. In the course of a frank discussion, we explained the circumstances which had given rise to the protests, and sought assurances that the dismissed men would be reinstated in the Force. The Archbishop, in turn, sought assurances that there would be no further meetings, and we gave him the best pledge possible, seeing that our primary concern was the reinstatement of the dismissed men.

At 9:00 am the following morning, November 13th the Archbishop saw Mr. Haughey and informed him of the previous night's work. Mr. Haughey was very pleased, and the Archbishop gave him a draft note outlining his views and asking him to release it soon. Mr. Haughey was not prepared to reinstate the dismissed men immediately, but agreed that they could be reinstated on making the required application. Archbishop McQuaid emphasised most emphatically how much the country depended on the good functioning, rather than on the discipline, of the Gardaí.

Things were now moving fast and it appears that the then Taoiseach, Mr.Lemass, had a hand in the affair. Mr. Haughey phoned the Archbishop at 10.15am to say that at the instigation of the Taoiseach it was decided to give a press conference announcing that the eleven dismissed men could, on application, be reinstated. This was apparently based on the draft note which Archbishop McQuaid had given to Mr. Haughey earlier that morning.

The following is the text of the press release:

> Through the intervention of Dr. McQuaid, Archbishop of Dublin, having obtained guarantees that no act of indiscipline would in future occur, I have decided to re-examine the arrangements whereby the Garda may express their views concerning conditions in the Force.

Dr. McQuaid pointed out to the Minister that he, Mr.Haughey, was the authority and that it was up to him to make the judgment, as he, the Archbishop, would say nothing to the newspapers on what had taken place.

The Archbishop then directed Father Fehily to secure complete acceptance of the guarantees already given to him. He records in his diary notes of the time that Father Fehily had reported that everything was being done to secure media silence, and that there would be no further protest meetings or committees.

Archbishop McQuaid continued to monitor the progress of what he had set in motion. Further meetings took place in the Dublin Institute for Catholic Sociology in Eccles Street, where the Archbishop met the dismissed men and those of us who had been involved in the negotiations. Later that evening, all those involved were called back to Eccles Street where the Archbishop explained that a committee of inquiry had been set up, and he read out its terms of reference. All of the dismissed men were to return to Garda Headquarters the following day for reinstatement.

The committee of inquiry set up as a result of the Archbishop's intervention comprised three members: Father Fehily, Michael Gill, Chairman of Gill Publishers, and Philip Cassidy, Secretary of J J

Jennings and Company, a prominent building firm in Dún Laoghaire.

Reformation at Last

There was still a long road to travel if the injustices, resentments and simmering discontent generated by the 1961 pay agreement were to be redressed.

The committee of inquiry made submissions, based largely on the experiences of Father Fehily and the Dublin Institute of Catholic Sociology. As far as I am aware, the committee's report was never made public, but its principle recommendations suggested root-and-branch reforms of the regulations governing the Representative Body. These recommendations were very much in line with the document which I had given to Assistant Commissioner Lincoln some two years previously.

In the drafting of new regulations, it was considered advisable to seek the views of the existing Representative Bodies. As the Garda rank had been primarily - indeed solely – involved, it followed that the views of the RBG should be sought. With Tony Coffey, my fellow Metropolitan delegate, we were brought officially into the concluding stages of drafting the proposals, and those who had been in control of the Representative Bodies were overlooked.

Tony Coffey was a big, likeable man from Connemara who joined the Force in 1939. He was elected to the Representative Body because of his sense of outrage over some of the ridiculous and annoying regulations then in force. Attached to the Traffic Department , he was a permanent fixture in College Green at that time. Controlling traffic from his busy point at the Bank of Ireland, he usually had a smile and a word for everyone – in hail, rain, or snow. He was, indeed, like his traffic point-duty colleagues, very much at the heart beat controlling Dublin traffic. He made the news when, by way of protest, he removed his tunic and draped it over a nearby traffic bollard, and continued to direct the traffic in his shirt sleeves. It was a very hot day in summer and the heat had, as we would say, gotten to him. But it was not just the heat. It was the frustration of the insensitive regulations that demanded the wearing of the uniform tunic at all times irrespective of weather conditions. So,

Tony decided there would be no more sweating it out on hot summer days. The Sunday Review carried a front-page photograph of him in shirt sleeves, minus his tunic, and the traffic bollard acting as a coat hanger. Not exactly an earth-shattering event, you might think, but, one of great importance to the Gardaí concerned. Shortly afterwards, the rules were changed, and henceforth traffic pointsmen across the city performed their summer duties in cool blue shirts and ties.

Following the successful intervention of Archbishop McQuaid and the reinstatement of the dismissed men, Tony and I spent days in negotiations at the Department of Justice. The drafting of new proposals that would give the Garda rank more independence and control was high on our agenda. In effect, the outcome of these negotiations was a basis for the new Representative Body Regulations. They were stepping-stones to the future. However, those were very difficult days for us, as we were very much on our own and without back-up from any source – other than advice and encouragement from Father Fehily. We were inexperienced in such matters and were negotiating with experienced civil servants. One cannot but wonder about the role of those who had been *de facto* in control of the affairs of the Representative Body. Not a word was uttered from that quarter. The Commissioner had shot his bolt by way of strong disciplinary action, and his role was now superfluous.

There was now an obligation on the Department of Justice officials to draft new proposals on representation. Such proposals would have to meet the changed circumstances, and obtain the support of the representatives of Garda rank. Therefore, our presence at the drafting of new proposals was imperative, and I believe that Tony and I played a useful and honourable role. We had set ourselves the solitary goal of setting up of an independent organisation for the Garda rank. Earlier experience had set me on this course, namely the domination which had been imposed by the Officer's Body and the failure of the RBG to assert its influence in the rejection of the Conciliation and Arbitration Scheme and the lack of support for a separate and independent assessment of the Scheme by the RBG. It was one of my long-held beliefs that the Gardaí would benefit greatly from the services of a professional adviser and I was determined that such a provision should be included in any new regulations. Such an approach seemed alien to Representative Body policy over the years. But to be fair to that earlier generation, the seeking of such assistance outside of the Force had been strictly prohibited. Indeed, on the occasion, in 1958, when I consulted with officers of the Irish Trade Union Congress, I was told that I would be dismissed if it came to the notice of my superiors.

The outcome of our discussions with officials from the Department of Justice was the drafting of new Representative Body Regulations. These were the stepping-stones that led to the statutory position of the Garda Representative Association (GRA).

Addressing the issue of new Representative Body Regulations in 1962, Charles Haughey told Dáil Éireann that the principal cause of discontent was the failure of the representative machinery. The new regulations provided that each group (rank) would sit separately and hold office for three years. Also, those committees could admit non-elected members to their meetings. He went on to explain that the Gardaí could have the full-time services of a Garda as their secretary and engage an outside consultant. These amendments to the regulations reflected the views of the Dublin Committee, and were those strongly advocated by Tony Coffey and myself in our discussions with the Department of Justice.

Mr. Haughey made clear that there was nothing to prevent any of the Representative Bodies from consulting as to the nature of a claim being brought under the Conciliation and Arbitration Scheme. Also the Garda Side was free to consult with the Representative Body as to whether or not a particular offer should be accepted. Further there could be free and open consultation, subject to the preservation of confidentiality. These latter words could, of course, become the classical get out clause for politicians and administrators wishing to play safe and cover their backs. Unfortunately, it could have the effect of negating the good purpose of what was originally intended. How, I wondered, could confidentiality be assured, while at the same time allowing free and open consultation? It had been left to the representatives of Garda rank to seek the reinstatement of the dismissed men and to seek reform of the Representative Body Regulations that would ensure fair and equitable representation for their members.

Enter Garret Fitzgerald

Some few months into our first year in the new office in Dublin Castle, we inserted an advertisement in the daily newspapers seeking the services of an economic consultant to advise the RBG on matters of pay, allowances and such matters. To our delight, one of the first to respond was Dr. Garret Fitzgerald, then an up-and-coming luminary and head of the private Economic Research Unit. We had discussions with Dr. Fitzgerald and it was agreed that he would become the Body's economic consultant at an agreed fee.

Dr. Fitzgerald was at that time chairman of the ESB General Arbitration Tribunal, as well as head of the Economic Research Unit, and we were naturally delighted to have secured the services of a man regarded as the country's leading financial expert. Our delight was short lived. Within weeks of his acceptance of the post, a somewhat embarrassed Dr. Fitzgerald returned to our office to say that he wished to withdraw from the agreement entered into some weeks earlier, as he was being asked to surrender his position on the ESB Arbitration Tribunal by the then Minister for Transport and Power, Mr. Erskine Childers. It had transpired that the Secretary to the Department, Dr. Thekla Beere, had raised the possibilities of a conflict of interests between his position as Chairman of the Arbitration Tribunal and as consultant to a quasi trade union Body. Dr. Fitzgerald was most apologetic, stating that he had no option but to withdraw from his agreement with the RBG.

We were naturally devastated by this turn of events. As a fledgling organisation, we lacked experience in financial matters, but realized the importance of discharging our mandate correctly. The provision of an independent office for the RBG had been our first success, which had not been achieved without some courage and determination on our part. It was essential that we continue to ensure the independence and status of the new Body, not to mention the need to be seen as fully capable of conducting our own affairs.

Dr. Fitzgerald's withdrawal was seen as a serious loss at a time when our major goal was the securing of a substantial pay rise for our members. We believed that the success or failure of the new Body depended on rectifying the injustices in the pay agreements of 1961. So, what was to be done about this early setback to our fortunes? Having given the matter serious consideration we concluded that we had no alternative but to seek redress at the highest level. We drafted a letter which I, as Chairman of the Body, would personally present to the Commissioner, while Jack Marrinan, as General Secretary, would deliver a copy to the Taoiseach, Mr. Lemass, who was also Acting Minister for Justice. We both realised that we were setting aside long-established procedures by going directly to Government. Indeed, this was precisely the view taken by Commissioner Costigan, but he nevertheless agreed to see me. I was ushered into the Commissioner's office, where I explained our concern over the issue of Dr. Fitzgerald's inability to take up the appointment.

Commissioner Costigan was clearly taken aback at what I told him. Having read the letter addressed to the Taoiseach, his first words were: "Do you mean to say that you have gone over my head to the head of Government?" My reply was, "I have to say that that is so, Sir. At this moment our General Secretary is in the course of delivering that letter to the Taoiseach." I was, of course, feeling a little nervous and uncomfortable in his presence. I realised that I was presenting the Commissioner with a *fait accompli*. Most likely, it was the first time ever that a member of Garda rank had done so. I have to say that Commissioner Costigan, while obviously upset, was most courteous and polite. On leaving the Commissioner, I returned to the office at Dublin Castle where we awaited the outcome of the afternoon's work.

Unfortunately, I do not have a copy of my letter to Mr. Lemass, but it should be on file at the GRA office in Phibsboro. Any documentation I made was of course properly deposited by me in the office at Dublin Castle, which I vacated in 1965. So I am now working entirely from personal recollections of events of over forty years ago. I do know that the letter to Mr. Lemass set out our serious objections to what we regarded as interference by the Minister for Transport and Power in the affairs of the Representative Body for Guards, and that the withdrawal of Dr. Fitzgerald would damage the morale of our members. No doubt, Mr. Lemass feared the possibility of a return to the serious discontent of November 1961. There would certainly have been no desire on anyone's part for a return to those days.

In any event, the letter had the desired effect. Some ten to fourteen days later, Dr. Fitzgerald called to our office and informed us that - to his surprise - Mr. Childers had just told him that the Taoiseach had directed him to take up the appointment with us. Garrett expressed astonishment at this turn of events and referred flatteringly to *whatever influences* we had brought to bear. We, for our part, were delighted to have succeeded in securing his services and to have passed our first serious test in asserting our independence. We assured Dr. Fitzgerald that he would be at no financial loss as a result of relinquishing his position with the ESB Arbitration Tribunal. In the event, we had no difficulty in obtaining approval from the Representative Body for an increase in Dr. Fitzgerald's fee, to equal that being paid by the ESB.

Before moving on from this historic episode, it is perhaps worthwhile to comment that had we not succeeded in retaining the services of Dr. Fitzgerald we would have suffered a serious setback. Not only would our standing with our members have suffered, but also we would have been seriously disadvantaged in the complex negotiations which lay ahead. After all, only a year had elapsed since the new RBG had been elected and placed in charge of its own affairs with its very own office in Dublin Castle.

In the light of the above, the following extract from Dr. Fitzgerald's memoir[*] may be of interest:

> In 1961 I was appointed Chairman of ESB General Arbitration Tribunal at £750 p.a. Two years later Joan saw an advertisement for Economic Consultant by the Representative Body for Guards, the organisation that was officially recognised as representing the basic rank for negotiating purposes. I applied and was appointed. Erskine Childers

---

[*] Garrett Fitzgerald, *All in a Life* p. 61 Macmillian 1991

called me in, with Department Secretary Dr. Thekla Beere, and pointed out the possible conflict with the position in the ESB. I agreed to tell the Representative Body for Guards immediately that I had to turn down their appointment. I regretted this outcome.

Ten days later I was called to Childers' office, and the embarrassed Tanaiste told me that the appointment with the RBG had led to near mutiny, since it was interpreted as evidence of Government interference at a time when there was already unrest in the Force. Childers went on to say that in the absence abroad of the recently appointed Minister for Justice, Mr. Charles J. Haughey, the Taoiseach had told him to direct me to take up the position that ten days earlier he had required me to turn down. I would of course have to resign from the Chairmanship of the ESB General Arbitration Tribunal.

I accepted this direction. The RBG, pleased to have down-faced the Government, were concerned that I should not be at a loss, and more than doubled their proposed fee, to the same level as that of the ESB Tribunal chairmanship."

Of further interest are the observations of Paddy Delaney.[*] The following brief extracts highlight the concern caused by this event:

The wholly unexpected resignation of Garrett Fitzgerald from his position as Chairman of the General Employees Tribunal in 1963 after a mere two years tenure was both a grievous disappointment and the occasion of considerable unease.

The Association had become aware of his appointment as Economic Consultant to the Garda Representative Body, but

since there was no immediate indication that this would affect his status on the Tribunal no problem was anticipated...In the

---

[*]Paddy Delaney and Micheál Ó Foghlú, *The Emergence of the Esboa: Two Perspectives* (ESB Officers Association)

Association's view, the resignation seemed unusually mystifying.

However, the possibility of ascertaining the true facts of the situation seemed quite remote.

With the publication in 1991, however, of Dr. Fitzgerald's memoirs, *All in a Life*, the true facts of this rather bizarre affair have at last come to light.

... Certainly, had the Association been in possession of firm evidence of the exercise of political pressure in this affair its reaction would not have been less rigorous than that of the Garda Representative Body.

In the light of the foregoing, it is interesting to speculate as to what might have happened had the ESBOA been fully aware of what lay at the heart of this matter. Would it have led to yet another strike in the ESB? Had we failed to retain the services of Dr. Fitzgerald, would the RBG have resigned in protest, thus perpetuating further serious unrest in the Force? Fortunately, both questions remained hypothetical. Dr. Fitzgerald proved an invaluable asset to our organisation. By the end of the summer, we had secured a major pay award and the future of the RBG was assured.

Nearly forty years later, in the course of a conversation with Dr. Fitzgerald, I asked him for his recollections about conditions in the Force at the time of his appointment. "I was appalled at your conditions," was his response. "You had two days off per month and no weekends. Appalling! I could not believe it!" On the matter of overtime he was not too happy either, feeling that if it were introduced it would change the character of the Force. He considered that a better solution might be found, possibly by way of financial compensation in basic pay structures, or increased monthly and annual leave.

If I recall correctly, Jack Marrinan and I held the view that the introduction of overtime would ensure a radical reduction in the number of hours which we were required to work at that time. The regulations stipulated a minimum of 48 hours per week but no maximum. In practice, members of the Force had no say in regard to their hours of duty. Regulations made by the Commissioner set the hours of duty and stated that leave was a privilege. The catch-phrase, "subject to the exigencies of the service" was a convenient escape hatch for the refusal of leave, for extending hours of duty, or for cancelling all leave. And there was no redress. We believed that the obligation to pay overtime would put a brake on abuses that were often imposed for no good or justifiable reason. We were, it has to be said, more concerned with ensuring fair conditions of service than simply increased earnings. Unfortunately, payment for overtime, when later introduced, became the subject of much acrimony, as the benefits were not always shared by those most deserving of them.

Following the reform of Representative Body Regulations, there was a great surge of interest in Representative Body affairs – an interest which had been sadly lacking until the controversial pay agreement of 1961. Not unnaturally perhaps, there emanated a degree of witch-hunting by some of the newly-elected members, who now perceived - rightly or wrongly - the possibility of malpractice in Representative Body affairs. Such perceptions were, I have to say, without foundation. Apart from some minor expenses, associated with attendance at half-yearly meetings, there was nothing in the way of monetary reward for members of the Representative Bodies. Minor expenses were sometimes recovered from sources such as the Garda Review or the Depot Canteen Stores. However, I did have some misgivings about the manner in which such expenses were disbursed. So much so, that on one occasion I made a point of personally donating a small disbursement of £5 to the funds of the newly-built Dominic Savio Boys' Club in Finglas, lest its official acceptance might in some way compromise my position. I wanted to assure my independence.

It must be remembered that there was no independent, voluntary source of funding for the Garda Representative Bodies. The State had total control – no meetings without official approval, no funds, and no question of voting rights for members of the Force. When collecting funds to support a legal case to secure the right to vote for members of the Garda Síochána, I was told that I was leaving myself open to disciplinary action.

In the first months of the new Representative Body for Guards, I perceived that - from time to time - a whiff of suspicion would arise when references were made to the former Representative Body. On one occasion, this bordered on McCarthyism. A member of the Body persisted in questioning me regarding the payment to me by cheque of £30 by the then General Secretary of the JRB. There was a very simple explanation. I had been responsible, on behalf of the Representative Bodies, for organising a reception for a visiting group of German police, and I was so embarrassed at the failure of the General Secretary to pay the account due to the hotel that I paid it myself. Months later, I got a refund from the General Secretary, and this was the cheque which had been trawled up by the energetic young member. In fairness, he may have thought that he had stumbled on some sort of scam which should be exposed.

I quote the incident as evidence of the aura of suspicion surrounding Representative Body affairs by younger members. While I had absolutely nothing to be concerned about, I felt embarrassed at the persistence with which the matter was pursued. We were very concerned to ensure that there would be complete openness in all matters, especially financial affairs.

Gaining access to financial resources was, of course, a major leap forward for the new RBG. Without such access, the road ahead would have proved extremely difficult. We had been denied financial resources since the foundation of the Force, and the Representative Bodies throughout the years were without the means to employ professional advice - which was, in any event, prohibited. When negotiating the drafting of new Representative Body Regulations, Tony Coffey and I strongly emphasised the right to solicit funds. Had we not secured this right, there would have been no Garret Fitzgerald, and no progress in achieving what we did for the organisation.

Towards a Better Future

Discussions took place in 1962 with the Dept. of Justice and Commissioner Costigan on setting up a new office for the RBG in Dublin Castle. In my view, it was of paramount importance that the new

Representative Body Regulations then being formulated should ensure the total independence of the RBG. As a means to this end, I deemed it essential that the administration and functioning of the new Body for the Garda rank should - as far as possible - be at one remove from officialdom. While the Commissioner had, in his response to the crisis which had arisen, made much of the generous provision by the State of offices and staff at John's Road, he seemed not to realise that perhaps this was part of the problem. I was convinced that new ground would have to be broken, if the Guards were ever to conduct their own affairs. After all, it was the old order which had contributed - however unconsciously - to the apathy and cynicism of the younger generation of Guards. It was the Garda rank, specially the junior members, which felt seriously aggrieved, and there could be no going back to the status quo. I was convinced that it was time for a new beginning.

In the course of these discussions, I had emphasized the importance of making provision in the regulations for a full-time General Secretary for the RBG. No such position was provided for, and I was only too well aware of what my own position, as Secretary of the RBG, had been for the previous two years that of a functionary devoid of power or authority and without any role or function. The JRB, administered from their official quarters at John's Road, had been the only source of representation. To my mind it went without saying that we should have a full-time General Secretary, and that the newly-elected Body should be provided with a suitable office from which it could properly function.

Commissioner Costigan asked me, as chairman of the newly-elected RBG, to come to his office to discuss the location of such an office. First of all, he suggested the provision of rooms at John's Road. I pointed out that this would defeat the stated aim of making a clean break from the past, and that I was totally opposed to such a solution. He then suggested rooms at the Garda Depot, but I stressed that, in order to emphasise a new beginning, a break with tradition would best serve all concerned. I felt that Commissioner Costigan was reluctant to break new ground on this issue and wished to maintain the traditional official control over what was being proposed. I considered the issue to be of considerable importance, and wished to emphasise this to the

Commissioner. I pointed out that failure to provide acceptable accommodation might result in the RBG deciding to seek accommodation in Liberty Hall. The suggestion of such a scenario had the desired effect, and some few days later the Commissioner offered us accommodation at Dublin Castle. This was acceptable, as it was perceived as being outside the orbit of past influences and offered the possibility of a fresh start, as well as presenting an independent image for the new Body.

That it was left to the lower ranks to bring about these changes was perhaps not surprising. As is usually the case, it is the foot-soldiers that are most disadvantaged in such circumstances. Reform seldom comes from above.

It may be of interest to observe here that the two rooms given to us by the Commissioner at Dublin Castle had a short time previously been refurbished and ear-marked for the Traffic Department - which already had accommodation on the ground floor. The Inspector in charge of Traffic, later to become Assistant Commissioner, was quite disturbed that he and his staff were being 'dispossessed.' Indeed, he made this quite clear to me by saying: "I won't be long about getting you fellows out of here!" I mention this to show that hurdles, large and small, were being encountered and not always from above. Fortunately, such attitudes were the exception rather than the rule.

The provision of an office, and the staffing of it, were of course essential to the goal of having our own independent organisation. It would not have been sufficient for the new Secretary to simply be given two rooms and nothing else. I had been elected Chairman of the new Body, with Jack Marrinan as full-time General Secretary. When it came to establishing the new office, the Body suggested that - because of my previous Representative Body experience - I could best give useful advice and guidance if I were to act as Assistant to the General Secretary during the initial period. As I had been deeply involved in Representative Body affairs for the previous five years, I agreed to full-time employment in the new office. Indeed, I welcomed the opportunity to continue to play a major part in Representative Body affairs. I was now being afforded an opportunity of full-time involvement, a position that I had been denied in 1958 under the old regime. Although there was no provision in the new regulations for this position, the Commissioner agreed to the Body's request that I be so employed. But the Commissioner did observe that such a position might be considered incompatible with my role as Chairman of the new Body. However, I assured him that I did not anticipate any difficulties in this regard, and that it was imperative that the new and inexperienced Body get off to the best possible start, uninfluenced by past events. Many years later it emerged that Commissioner Costigan was very well aware of the tensions and difficulties that existed in the Dublin Metropolitan Area regarding the Representative Body, especially the efforts being made by the Dublin Committee to have a say in its affairs. Unfortunately, Commissioner Costigan had other difficulties at the time and was unwilling to stir up a hornet's nest by taking on Chief Superintendent Collins and other entrenched senior officers, with whom he was having his own problems. Had he taken the earlier opportunity, which was within his grasp, of supporting the efforts of the Dublin Committee, perhaps he would have been spared a lot of pain.

As time progressed, we made friends and contacts with a broad spectrum of all ranks at both administrative level and throughout the country. Our immediate and most important objective was the formulation and presentation of a pay claim, which would rectify the anomalies that had arisen as a result of recent pay awards, and which would secure for Guards remuneration and status commensurate with their role in society. It was, of course, essential for the success of the new organisation that the perceived injustices and sense of alienation generated by recent events were clearly redressed. We were determined that the best possible lines of communication should be maintained with those we represented. District, Divisional, and Area Committees were set up, as provided for under the new Representative Body Regulations (1962). By means of a monthly Broadsheet we kept them fully informed, while stimulating their interest in the organisation. In the light of past Representative Body policy, or lack of same, this was somewhat radical. Times were changing, and it was no longer acceptable that the occasional circular from Headquarters would suffice. The Gardaí were now - for the first time - being kept fully informed on aspects of pay, formulation of policy, meetings at all levels, and of any progress being made. In addition, we had the task of establishing good relationships with kindred organisations and of getting on with the task of building an organisation that might command the respect of our adversaries, as well as the loyalty of our members.

Jack Marrinan and I had contested the election for the position of full-time General Secretary at the initial meeting of the new Body. Jack proved the victor, and by unanimous agreement it was proposed that I accept the position of Chairman. I have to say that in view of the fact that I had been associated with the old regime it was not too surprising that I did not succeed to the post of General Secretary. I was gratified, nevertheless, that I had topped the poll in my own District, been elected to the new RBG, been proposed for the position of its first full-time General Secretary, and unanimously voted in as its first Chairman. Having regard to all that had occurred, I was happy, not only to accept the position of Chairman, but also to serve in the new office which we had secured at Dublin Castle. I wished to pursue the ideal of a truly independent organisation and its implementation of the reforms which we had unsuccessfully striven to attain since 1958. Jack Marrinan proved a tenacious and resourceful General Secretary, and we established a good working relationship until my term of office ended in 1965.

As already stated, the new pay claim was a priority. Dr. Garrett Fitzgerald was an invaluable asset. Always a great man for statistics, he kept us busy researching information on a wide variety of issues which he wished to incorporate in the pay claim. We had frequent meetings with him to consider suggestions and to monitor progress. With the support and goodwill of many Guards and other ranks, the new District Committees assisted in gathering statistical data that would not have been otherwise available. It must also be said that staff at Headquarters were generally most agreeable and responsive to our many requests, which frequently necessitated considerable delving into official records. Together with the work on the pay claim, there was the task of developing the new Body along lines envisaged in the course of the negotiations, all of which led to radical reform and the promulgation of new Representative Body Regulations in 1962.

Secretarial facilities were of the most basic kind – a typewriter, a filing cabinet, a desk and some tables and chairs supplied from official sources. For the production and distribution of our monthly Broadsheet we were largely dependent on the goodwill of others for the use of the Gestetner machine at the Criminal Records Office across the yard. We now had access to our own funds and were in a position to purchase our own supplies of coloured printing paper and other stationary.

Insignificant as such things might seem to-day, it was indeed a considerable leap forward for the Gardaí to be in control of their own affairs, to the extent that funds were becoming available, and that for the first time a General Secretary was empowered to function full-time on their behalf. Circumstances had now changed dramatically from the days when I endeavoured to function as Secretary while on full-time regular police duties at Dún Laoghaire. The Representative Body offices at John's Road were in those days most definitely not within the domain of the Secretary of the RBG. Indeed, Commissioner Costigan, when endeavouring to justify the dismissals in 1961, chose to ignore this reality by claiming that the State was funding the cost of the office at John's Road.

Following the election of a new RBG in 1962, the views of members of Garda rank on a new pay claim were sought through the newly elected Committees. For the first time, members were being given the opportunity to have a voice in their own conditions of service. It was also an opportunity to offset some of the damage occasioned by the perceived arbitrary manner in which past decisions had been taken. The ultimate test for this fledgling organisation would, of course, be the outcome of the new pay claim. The claim came before the new Conciliation Council, to which each of the three Representative Bodies now had independent and separate access. Not unexpectedly, there was no agreement, and the claim then went to the newly-appointed Arbitration Board.

Jack Marrinan and I were the Garda members on the Arbitration Board. The Chairman was Mr. Justice Fred Mangan, whose appointment we had proposed and successfully pursued, notwithstanding opposition from the Department of Justice, which until then had its nominee more or less automatically accepted. But we were determined to have our say in the light of changed circumstances. Mr. Mangan was a popular and respected Justice of the Dublin District Court. He sat in No. 2 Court at the Bridewell and was therefore very well known to most Gardaí who were at the forefront of regular police work in Dublin. We felt that Mr. Mangan had first-hand knowledge of conditions for the average Garda, that he would have a deep understanding of their difficulties, and that he was well placed to make a fair and realistic assessment of any case being made on their behalf.

There was some difficulty is securing official approval for Mr Mangan's appointment as Chairman of the Arbitration Board. It was breaking new ground for us to actually submit a nomination for the position, as this had until then been regarded as the prerogative of the Departments of Justice and Finance. The Official Side were anxious to continue with the previous Chairman, Mr. Liston SC, and the matter had dragged on for some months in the absence of an agreement. I recall that during the course of a Conciliation Council meeting the then Secretary of the Department of Justice, Peter Berry, who was Chairman of the Council, had politely suggested over coffee that I might use my influence to secure agreement on Mr. Liston's appointment. How things had now changed!

In any event, Mr. Mangan was appointed Chairman of the Arbitration Board. The pay claim was heard in the summer of 1963 and the award in August proved a gigantic leap forward in establishing the future benchmark of Garda pay. It reflected major changes in the pay scale of Gardaí and redressed the mistakes of the Conciliation Agreement of 1961. He awarded increases in pay of up to 25%.

I have often reflected on Mr. Mangan and what he did for us. In my opinion, the Garda Síochána should forever honour his memory. As Chairman of the Arbitration Board in 1963, at which the Garda rank had for the first time stood alone and independent, he redressed the serious mistakes that had been made in the 1961 Conciliation Council Pay award. More importantly, he gave to the Force a status within the public service which it justly deserved. Not since 1923 had the Garda Síochána been given the status that was their due.

Mr. Mangan's award was very well received. Satisfaction with our efforts was widely expressed, and there was a general feeling of goodwill towards the new Body. It was now seen as the premier Body for the advancement of working conditions in the Force.

For my own part, I was happy that much of what we had striven for over the years had at last come to pass. I was indeed satisfied to have played a part in this success, and looked forward to the achievement of greater things. When the term of the reformed RBG expired in 1965, new elections were held. Although successful in being elected at District level and to the Dublin Committee, I was not voted onto the RBG. New faces had arrived on the scene, with the result that others took my place. Having been chairman and - with Jack Marrinan - one of the two Garda representatives on the Arbitration Board, the likelihood that I would not continue for at least another while had not crossed my mind.

The reforms and achievements of those early years were the foundation stones of the GRA. The eventual establishment of offices at Phibsboro, with full-time paid staff, was indeed a far cry from Commissioner Costigan's fears when I presented him with the possibility that the newly-elected Representative Body for Guards might feel obliged to seek offices in Liberty Hall!

Whatever experience I may have contributed, and however valuable this may have been, it had served its purpose. Reluctantly, I had no option but to vacate the office at Dublin Castle and return to ordinary duty at Dun Laoghaire. I was, of course, very disappointed at this unexpected turn of events. But the past is another country.

I have got immense pleasure from writing this memoir. For me it has been a wonderful journey through a panorama of memories. Perhaps, also, I have shed a little light on some of the lesser known aspects of life in the Garda Síochána.

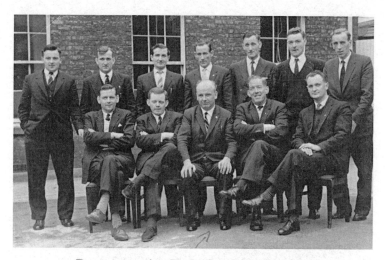

Representative Body for Guards, 1962

Seated: P. Nolan, J. Marrinan (Secretary), E. Gunn (Chairman), C. Ryan, J. Fitzgerald.
Standing: P. Courtney, N. Scott, P. Lally, J. Scott, J. Lee, M. Harlow, R. Keating.

The inauguration of Conciliation and Arbitration Scheme – 1958

Seated: L to R: Insp. H. Nangle, Chief Supt. T. Collins, Commissioner D. Costigan,
Deputy Commissioner G. Brennan, Assistant Commissioner T. Woods.
Standing: Supt D. Corcoran, Garda M. Eagan, E. Gunn, Sgt. D. Fingelton,
Chief Supt. T. McCarthy.

The Garda Side Conciliation Council – 1958

L to R: Supt D. Corcoran, Garda M. Egan, Garda E. Gunn, Chief Supt T. Collins,
Sgt D, Fingelton, Insp H. Nangle

Dún Laoghaire Garda Station – prior to its demolition in 1992

Main Street, Pomeroy – 1920s

Manorhamilton Football Team

The Sligo Leitrim & Northern Counties Railway

Manorhamilton Workhouse – from a painting by Marie McDonald